Wood Pellet Smoker Grill Cookbook 2021

AF256339

Learn To Make Easy, And Healthy Smoker Grill Recipes To Make Your Food Parties Memorable

Harrison Cohen

Table Of Content

© **Copyright 2021 by Harrison Cohen - All rights reserved.**

The following Book is reproduced below with the goal of providing information that is as accurate and reliable as possible. Regardless, purchasing this Book can be seen as consent to the fact that both the publisher and the author of this book are in no way experts on the topics discussed within and that any recommendations or suggestions that are made herein are for entertainment purposes only. Professionals should be consulted as needed prior to undertaking any of the action endorsed herein.

This declaration is deemed fair and valid by both the American Bar Association and the Committee of Publishers Association and is legally binding throughout the United States.

Furthermore, the transmission, duplication, or reproduction of any of the following work including specific information will be considered an illegal act irrespective of if it is done electronically or in print. This extends to creating a secondary or tertiary copy of the work or a recorded copy and is only allowed with the express written consent from the Publisher. All additional right reserved.

The information in the following pages is broadly considered a truthful and accurate account of facts and as such, any inattention, use, or misuse of the information in question by the reader will render any resulting actions solely under their purview. There are no scenarios in which the publisher or the original author of this work can be in any fashion deemed liable for any hardship or damages that may befall them after undertaking information described herein.

Additionally, the information in the following pages is intended only for informational purposes and should thus be thought of as universal. As befitting its nature, it is presented without assurance regarding its prolonged validity or interim quality. Trademarks that are mentioned are done without written consent and can in no way be considered an endorsement from the trademark holder.

Introduction

Pellet grills have quickly become the hottest trend in the grilling and BBQ world. People are excited about the new attributes and conveniences that pellet grills bring to the market, especially since technology in the industry hasn't changed much over the last 30 years or so. However, understanding how they work is necessary in order to fully appreciate everything they have to offer. Pellet grills could be best described as outdoor cookers, which combine characteristics of smokers, charcoal and gas grills, and ovens into one unit. Pellet grills can provide direct or indirect heat because they use 100% natural hardwood pellets as a fuel source. There are so many different types of grills as well as smokers on the market that choosing the right one for you can be difficult. Wood pellet grills, on the other hand, cook differently as compared to traditional propane, gas and charcoal grills. Wood pellet grills add a smoky flavor to your food that you can't get anywhere else by using pellets that are made of compacted wood and sawdust.

The true advantage of buying a pellet grill is the high quality plus the flavor of the food you can prepare on it. The best flavor comes from wood, which is why professional barbecue chefs use it. And, unlike charcoal or gas, you can customize the flavor of your wood pellets by mixing and matching them to achieve the best flavor for whatever you cook on your grill. Using only high-quality pellets has a number of advantages. They produce the best flavor, first and foremost. Second, they produce less ash, requiring less cleanup. Finally, high-quality pellets burn more evenly, for longer periods of time, and with greater efficiency. The truth is that the best barbecue is done over a wood fire rather than propane or natural gas. Food smoked on a propane grill simply does not taste the same. Furthermore, propane cooks your food too hot to provide authentic BBQ flavor and dries it out. So, if you're new to pellet grilling or smoking and are wondering how pellet grills work, this is a must-read book for you because, in addition to training you about the numerous uses and benefits of wood pellet grills, this book will also help you improve your cooking skills by providing a great collection of pellet grill cooking recipes.

CHAPTER 1: Uses & Benefits of Wood Pellet Grill

Pellet grills are often misunderstood by backyard grillers as being only for hardcore professionals. However, if you're undecided about which grill to buy, pellet grills provide a simple, clean, and consistent way to cook a wide variety of foods along with great wood flavor. Pellet grilling is less difficult than you might think. Pellet grills, as the name implies, burn tiny pellets that are sold in a number of different hardwoods to produce subtle flavor differences. These pellets are poured into the pellet hopper on the grill and fed to the fire pot via an auger. The fire pot itself creates fire with the help of fans and an igniter, which is then controlled by a digital controller. There are no unexpected flare-ups or unexpected temperature changes.

As a result, you won't have to be concerned about over-smoking your food. Many grillers opt for a pellet grill because it combines the convenience as well as cleanliness of propane with the flavor and aroma of wood-fired cooking. Smoker grills are usually versatile. Some models combine a grill and a smoker into one unit. It's a space-saving and cost-effective combination. Pellet grills have extremely precise temperature control, allowing them to cook at temperatures ranging from 180 to 500 degrees Fahrenheit. This enables the backyard chef to do everything from slow smoking briskets to searing steaks, preparing hamburgers, and serving seafood. You'll be surprised at the range of foods you could even prepare, including desserts. There are several steel versions with dual-wall construction available on the market. The design traps thermal energy inside while keeping the outside temperature out. Because pellet grills are so good at controlling heat, you can use them any day of the year, even in the middle of the winter, and know that the temperature inside the lid will be consistent.

1.1 How do Pellet Grills work?

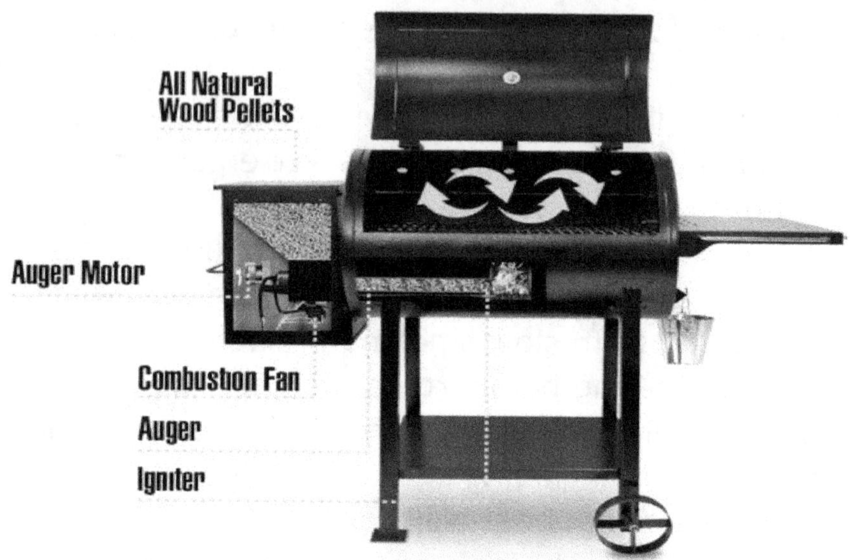

Wood pellets are loaded into a hopper, which serves as a storage container. An auger powered by electricity then feeds the pellets into a cooking chamber. The wood pellets ignite through combustion, heating the cooking chamber. The air is then drawn in through intake fans. After that, the heat and smoke are spread throughout the cooking area. Pellet grills, like ovens, allow you to control the temperature digitally or with a dial, usually ranging from 180°F to 500°F. As a result, you have the option of cooking "low and slow" or "searing hot." The meat's internal temperature can be monitored using a meat probe that connects to the control board on most pellet grills. There are grills that use a patented plate that provides indirect or direct heat, as well as eight different cooking options.

1.2 How to start a pellet grill?

When checking for gas in the truck, as with any road trip, the first thing you should do is double-check that you have plenty of pellets in the hopper. As a general standard, you can have 2 lbs. of pellets per hour of low and slow smoking or 4 lbs. per hour of high and fast grilling. It is relatively simple to start a pellet smoker grill. Begin by following these simple instructions to set up your smoker grill:

- Make sure the hopper is full of high-quality wood pellets.

- Inspect the firebox for cleanliness and leave the door and lid open.

- Connect your smoker to an electrical outlet.

- Turn on the device by pressing the power button. You should hear the party started.

The first few pellets may take a few minutes to ignite, but smoke will begin to appear. Keep the door open until the smoke has cleared, which could take up to 3-5 minutes. The sound of fire will soon be heard. The temperature should then gradually rise. Close the door or lid and raise the temperature of your smoker to the desired level once the smoke has cleared. Before putting meat into the smoker or smoker grill, allow the unit to reach and maintain that temperature.

1.3 Why pellet grills?

In a pellet grill, everything gets infused with a real wood smoky flavor when hardwood pellets are burned. Because pellet grills have fan-forced convection, they can be used with either direct or indirect heat. This means that no matter what happens, hot, smoky air will continue to circulate inside the grill, creating an even cloud of flavor. You could even smoke foods low and slow for hours, in addition to adding smoky flavors. Some professional chefs even leave the grills unattended for hours at a time while at work or sleeping at night to achieve perfectly smoked foods without having to babysit them. This makes smoking even the most difficult cuts, such as brisket, a breeze. When brisket is cooked, everyone loves it; now you can enjoy it while cooking it as well. To do so, simply set up your grill as directed in the "Pellet Grill Setup" section, turn it on "smoke," and monitor the progress with a remote thermometer or a meat probe.

1.4 Pellet grill vs. smoker

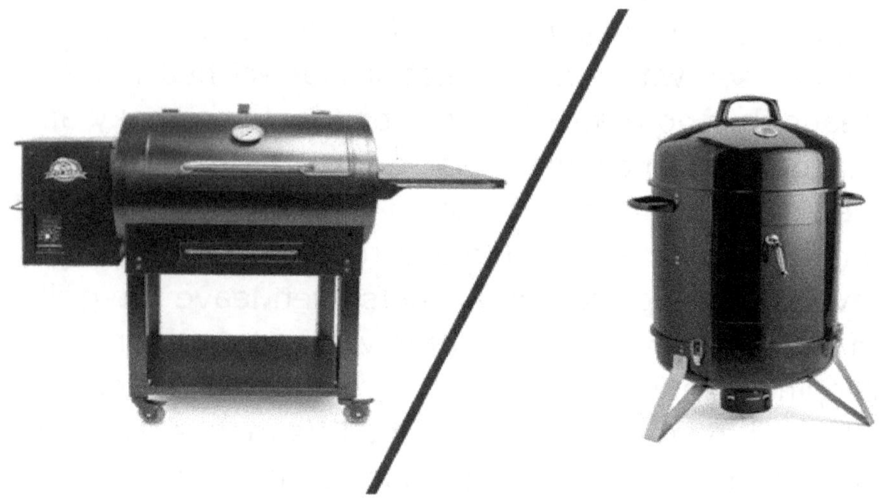

Pellet grills offer the option of smoking foods, but they differ from traditional smokers in a few ways. Pellet grills, in particular, are much easier to control temperatures than traditional smokers because they use an automated fuel as well as air delivery system.

1.5 Pellet grill vs. propane (gas) grills

Consumers will appreciate the convenience of both gas and pellet grills. However, there are some significant differences between the two grill types. Gas grills are ideal for cooking at temperatures ranging from medium to high. Gas grills, on the other hand, typically do not perform well at low temperatures due to poor insulation.

1.6 Pellet grill vs. charcoal

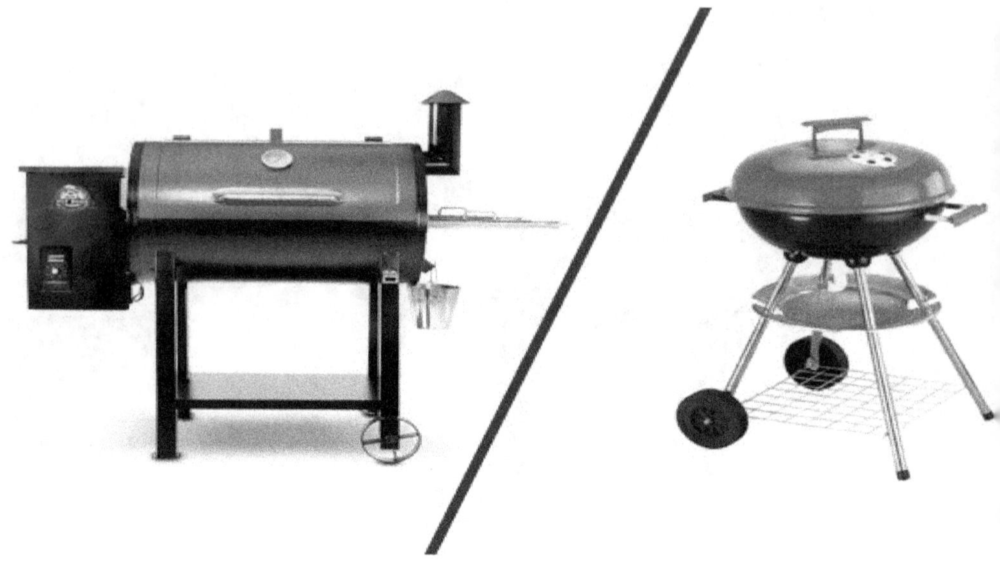

Cooking on a charcoal grill is a time-consuming process that requires a lot of practice. This is because controlling temperatures on a charcoal grill can be difficult. Pellet grills are appealing because they provide an even simpler method of temperature control. They're also a lot easier to clean up as compared to charcoal grills because a 40-pound bag of wood pellets only produces about 12 cups of ash.

1.7 How to cook with wood pellets?

There would be no need to be concerned if you didn't cook with a wood pellet smoker before. It's important to understand the basics if you didn't cook with wood pellets before. But once you've mastered those, you will be a wood pellet expert.

Wood-fired taste with wood-fired ease

The truth is that the perfect outdoor cooking can be done on a wood fire grill, which gives significantly more flavor as compared to a natural gas grill or propane. Food smoked on a propane grill simply does not taste the same. Furthermore, propane cooks your food too hot to provide genuine BBQ seasoning and dries it out. Cooking on a pellet grill as well as a smoker allows you to set specific temperatures and then forget about it as your food cooks.

How do grill with wood pellets work?

You've probably had hickory-smoked BBQ as well as wood-fired pizza, but until now, there hasn't been a simple method to get those flavors to your backyard. With the introduction of the wood pellet, cooking with hardwood has not been easier, cleaner, or more suitable. And the taste of hardwood is unrivaled. It is now much easier to deliver a specific quantity of hardwood into a grill to be burned in a controlled way by reducing pure hardwood to sawdust and compressing it into uniform, food-grade pellets.

Different flavor with different pellet

	BEEF	PORK	POULTRY	SEAFOOD	VEGGIES
MESQUITE	●		●		
HICKORY	●	●	●		
APPLE		●	●		●
CHERRY		●	●	●	●
PECAN	●	●	●		
COMPETITION BLEND	●	●	●	●	●

You can easily get mesquite salmon, hickory-smoked pork chops, or any other flavor. To release the pellets, just put a basket under the grill hopper and open the trap door. With little effort, you can add up the new flavor. By mixing your favorite flavors, you can exercise your creativity and experiment, for instance, pecan and cherry or oak and apple. The ability to infuse the foods with delicate or intense flavors is part of the fun of grilling with pellets.

The mechanism of smoking and grilling with wood pellets

You're making life pretty easy when you grill and smoke with wood pellets in the backyard. Most grills are built in such a way that it's simple to move wood pellets from the hopper to the grill, letting you achieve the desired temperature with minimal effort.

1.8 Avoid temperature variations as you cook with wood pellets

You should get consistent results and minimal temperature variation if you buy the best quality wood pellets.

Premium Benefits of Grilling and Smoking Meat

Since man learned how to make fire, people have been smoking meat. There are a variety of reasons why this cooking method has stood the test of time and is used in almost every culture on earth. There are numerous advantages to smoking meat.

Flavor

Smoking imparts a unique taste that cannot be replicated by other methods of cooking, like grilling or baking. Smoking meat "low and slow" breaks down collagen- it is a protein found in muscle tissue- resulting in much more tender meat. It also melts fat, which also combines with tender meat to create a truly delectable meal. The meat's flavor is also augmented by the aromas produced by smoking.

Enhanced Smell and Appearance

By enhancing the aroma of the smoke, the hardwoods used as fuel also help to add flavor to the meat. Chemicals form cellulose and lignin when the wood is burned. The main hardwoods used in smoking are:

- Mesquite
- Pecan
- Apple
- Oak
- Hickory
- Maple
- Alder
- Cherry

Distinct aromas are released into the smoke depending on the type of hardwood used, which also eventually permeates into the meat as it cooks, introducing a variety of different flavors to the meat. Smoking also leaves an acidic coating on the meat that is quite tasty as well as gives it a distinct look and texture. A pink smoke ring should appear just inside this coating if done correctly. Pit masters and chefs all over the world seek out the smoke ring as a signature sign of properly smoked meats.

Meat Preservation

Prehistoric cavemen used to hang the meat in the caves to dry it out and store it. The smoke would loom as well as slowly cook the food storage because these caves and huts lacked chimneys. As a result, our forefathers discovered by accident that smoking preserved their food faster than conventional methods. They liked the flavor as well.

Food Safety

Because of the lack of moisture in the meat at the end of the smoking process, as well as the acidic coating, bacteria have a difficult time surviving. Bacteria cannot enter the meat because of the coating, and if they do, the dry environment makes it hard for bacteria to stay alive and multiply.

Cooking on pellet grills is fun

It's in our DNA to smoke food. We've been doing it for centuries, and as a result, we can't get enough of the sight and smell of a fire. The aroma created by those two elements fills our senses with a primitive delight. We not only like smoke on its own, but we also like it when it's combined with meat. Bringing family and friends together for a day in the backyard for smoking ribs or brisket smoking is the ideal way to bring people together.

Cooking on pellet grills is good for your health

It turns out that smoking and slow cooking imparts a unique flavor to less tender meat cuts and leaner meat, too. Because lean meats have a lower caloric value and much less fat, they can aid in the development of lean muscle mass. Because recent studies have suggested that using meats filled with preservatives can cause cancer, it's better to stick with uncured and raw meats for the smoking process. Low-and-slow cooking of turkey, fish, game meat and chicken can be a great way to get more lean protein into your diet.

It offers versatility

You can smoke almost any type of meat, as well as salts, fruits, vegetables, sugars, oils and spices, to add flavor elements that could be lacking. Pellet grills can easily do everything from grilling hot dogs to slow smoking a rib roast.

Efficiency

For every 20 pounds of pellets, you could indeed cook for around 20 hours. Pellets can cost anywhere from $15 to $20 per bag, depending on the brand and where you buy them. When you do the math, pellet cooking is usually less expensive than a comparably-sized gas grill.

Value

Pellet grills made of stainless-steel components as well as backed by a 4-year warranty can be more expensive than the everyday grill you'll find at a big box store. If you're looking to buy a grill, you'll come across grills that are priced to maximize value over quality.

You eat less fat

You eat less fat when you grill because the fat drips off the grates. Consider the difference between cooking a burger on the grill than in a pan on the stove. The fat renders on the grill. Because the fat in a pan on the cook top has nowhere to go, it pools and is ultimately absorbed by the meat.

Vegetables on the grill are better for you

Most people are unaware that when vegetables are grilled, they retain more vitamins and minerals. This is particularly true of vegetables with low water content. Furthermore, vegetables tossed on the grill are typically fresh and in season, and this is a step up from canned vegetables. Cooking your vegetables in this manner, whether wrapped in tin foil or simply placed on top of the grill, is nutritionally superior to boiling or frying.

You use less butter
You'll have juicy cuts of meat as well as tasty vegetables if you master the grill and don't overcook your food. You'll be less likely to reach for the butter and other condiments to spice up your food because the grill locks in more moisture. Not only do you consume fewer calories, but you also consume fewer unhealthy substances.
Avoid heating up the home

During the summer, it can be challenging to bake roasts and casseroles in the oven. As the air conditioner tries to cool down the house, the oven could even quickly heat up the interior setting, increasing your energy bills. When you smoke outside before coming back inside, you could even keep the house cool and comfortable.

1.9 The Benefits of Smoking Meat with a Pellet Grill

The ease and convenience with which Pellet Grills make the smoking process are one of the reasons they have taken the barbecue world by storm. The smoking craze isn't just a neighborhood brawl over who has the most expensive grill. Smoking meat alters the way it cooks and has a significant impact on the whole flavor. Smoking meat for a longer span causes collagen-it is a hard muscle tissue protein-to breakdown, making the meat tender. When meat is simply grilled, this effect does not occur. The flavor of the meat is also affected by the smoke from the wood, which changes the internal color of the meat to a light pink as the smoke is absorbed into the muscle tissue. When the meat is tasted, the benefits of smoking become obvious, but it's possible that this trend has only recently caught on because smoking isn't as simple as it appears. For instance, smoking most foods necessitates an even longer cook time and greater attention to the grill temperature. That is why many grill manufacturers have spent time developing grills that monitor and automate smoke input as well as temperature.

Better temperature control

Because the strength of the fire varies as the wood burns, regular smokers may experience extreme temperature swings. Because wood pellet grills insulate as well as circulate heat more effectively, there are fewer heat fluctuations and a consistent temperature throughout the cooking process.

You don't need separate equipment for different types of cooking

Pellet grills provide the most versatility in terms of cooking. Pellet grills can be used for a variety of purposes, including smoking, barbecuing, roasting, charring, broiling, baking, grilling and more.

You don't have to constantly feed fuel to the fire

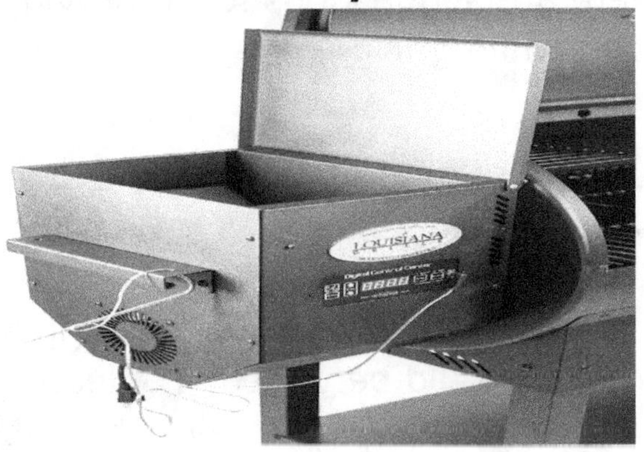

Pellet grills store pellets and then feed them into a burn pot when the temperature inside the grill begins to drop. This allows the grill to maintain its temperature without the need for the user to continually add pellets. Even on long smokes for meat cuts like brisket or pork shoulder, a full 20-pound capacity hopper must give you around 20 hours of cook time, so you can literally set it and forget it.

1.10 Tips for healthy grilling

Given below are a few tips to make the next meal even healthier before you fire up the grill for tonight's dinner. Here are suggestions for improving your family's diet while grilling.

Buy lean meats

Whereas the cheeseburgers are a grilling staple, your outdoor menu should be varied. Try lean meat cuts such as chicken, fish, or pork. Pick the leanest beef you could even find when you're craving a burger. Look for the number 93/7 on the package. That means only 7% is fat. The healthier the meat is, the leaner it is.

Grill your veggies

Every meal should include vegetables, so throw some peppers or zucchini on the grill while you're grilling. As a side dish, try grilling sweet corn as well as making veggie kabobs. Another nutrient-rich addition that many people enjoy is a spinach salad with a light vinaigrette dressing.

Marinate your meats

Who doesn't like a steak marinated in honey garlic glaze or pork chops with lemon pepper? The great news is that marinating not only enhances the flavor of your meal but may also benefit your health. There are some worries about cancer-causing chemicals spilling into the meat when cooked at high temperatures or over charcoal. Marinating the meat, on the other hand, is thought to help remove these chemicals from the meat by up to 99 percent.

Try healthy alternatives

If burgers, as well as steak, are your go-to grilling choices, then this book is the best choice for you to look for ideas. For the grill, there are a plethora of inventive and surprising recipes. Have you ever attempted to make a pizza on the grill, for example? It's a possibility. To grill something other than beef, pick up some whole-wheat dough at the store, preheat the grill, and add some sauce and vegetables. While grilling is usually associated with summer, you can also use a small electric grill indoors as the weather begins to cool and the seasons change. It'll keep you going until you can fire up the grill again.

CHAPTER 2: Wood Pellet Grill Seafood Recipes

We have collected a number of delicious food recipes in this chapter that you will enjoy cooking on your wood pellet grill.

2.1. Grilled Shrimp with Old Bay and Aioli

Preparation time

35 minutes

Servings

4 persons

Ingredients

We have listed below the ingredients that would be required by you for cooking the healthy and tasty meal:

- ½ cup + 1 tablespoon canola oil, for the grill
- 1 lb. shell-on shrimp (16–25 per pound)
- 3 finely grated garlic cloves, divided
- 1½ teaspoon Old Bay seasoning for serving
- ¾ teaspoon kosher salt, divided
- 1 egg yolk
- 2 lemons, cut

Instructions

Given below are the detailed instructions for cooking this tasty meal. You need to follow these instructions in the given order.

- Prepare a grill for moderate-high heat. Lightly oil grate.
- Place the shrimp in a medium mixing dish. Toss in 1 Tablespoon oil, 2/3 of the garlic, 1½ teaspoon Old Bay,

and 3/4 teaspoon salt. Allow 10–15 minutes to rest while you make the aioli.

- In a medium mixing dish, whisk together the egg yolk and the remaining garlic. 1 teaspoon lemon zest, finely grated into the egg mixture. Stir in the remaining 1/2 cup oil in a steady stream until the mixture is dense and pale yellow. Half a lemon juice should be added at this stage. Season to taste with salt—it should have a cheerful flavor.

- Half the left lemon. Grill the shrimp and 3 lemon halves (cut sides down) for 1–2 minutes, or until the shells are nicely browned and crispy in some places, the flesh is opaque, and the cut sides of the lemons are deeply caramelized.

- On a serving platter, spread the aioli. Arrange the fried shrimp and lemons on top. Season with a pinch of Old Bay.

2.2 Lobster Tails with Basil-Lemon Butter

Preparation time

21 minutes

Servings

4 persons

Ingredients

We have listed below the ingredients that would be required by you for cooking the healthy and tasty meal:

- 1 tablespoon fresh lemon juice

- ¼ teaspoon hot pepper sauce

- Butter

- 1¼ cup (2 1/2 sticks) unsalted butter

- 2 tablespoons finely chopped fresh basil leaves

- 1 tablespoon finely grated lemon zest

- A half teaspoon kosher salt

- 4 lobster tails, each 6 to 10 ounces

Instructions

Given below are the detailed instructions for cooking this tasty meal. You need to follow these instructions in the given order.

- Preheat the grill to medium heat (350° to 450°F) for direct cooking.

- Melt the butter in a small saucepan at low heat, swirling the pan occasionally. Skim the foam off the top of the melted butter and discard it

- Heat for at least one minute soon after inserting the butter ingredients

- Turn off the heat. One-quarter cup of the butter should be reserved for grilling the lobster. To maintain the remaining butter warm for serving, cover the saucepan

- Brush some of the butter retained for grilling on the meat side of the lobster. Grill the lobster tails, meat side down, for 2 to 3 minutes, depending on size, over direct medium heat with the lid closed. Brush the tops of the shells with a little more butter, turn them over, and grill for another 5 to 8 minutes, or until the meat is white and firm but not dry. Remove the lobster from the grill as well as serve immediately with the reserved butter

2.3 Grilled Fish

Preparation time

20 minutes

Servings

4 persons

Ingredients

We have listed below the ingredients that would be required by you for cooking the healthy and tasty meal:

- Kosher salt
- Freshly ground black pepper
- 1 tsp. chili powder
- 1 tsp. dried oregano
- 1/4 tsp. cayenne pepper
- 1 1 1/2"-thick fillet skin-on white fish, such as bass or cod
- Lime wedges, for serving

Instructions

Given below are the detailed instructions for cooking this tasty meal. You need to follow these instructions in the given order.

- Preheat the grill to high heat. Combine chili powder, oregano, cayenne, and salt and pepper in a mixing bowl
- Season the fish with the spice mixture all over

- Cook for eight to ten minutes, skin-side down, until almost completely opaque throughout

- Cook for another 2 to 3 minutes on the other side, or until opaque throughout

2.4 Salmon with Grilled Lemons and Yogurt Sauce

Preparation time

53 minutes

Servings

4 persons

Ingredients

We have listed below the ingredients that would be required by you for cooking the healthy and tasty meal:

- 2 tsp. Fresh dill, finely chopped
- ¼ tsp. Sriracha
- ¼ tsp. Lemon zest, finely grated
- ¼ tsp. kosher salt
- 1 tbsp. olive oil
- ¾ c. whole-milk Greek-style yogurt
- 1 minced garlic clove
- 1 tsp. soy sauce
- 1 tbsp. fresh lime juice
- Black pepper, ground
- Dill sprigs
- One large lemon, seeds removed, (¼") thick,
- 1 tsp. honey

- 4 salmon fillets (with skin), each (6 - 8 oz.) and (1 - 1¼″) thick, bones removed

- ½ tsp. Sriracha

- Salt

Instructions

Given below are the detailed instructions for cooking this tasty meal. You need to follow these instructions in the given order.

- Whisk together the sauce ingredients in a bowl.

- In a bowl, stir together the marinade material.

- Coat the flesh sides liberally with the marinade and season with salt as well as pepper. Allow for 15 - 30 minutes at room temperature before serving.

- Place the lemon wedges on a dish as well as coat with some of the leftover marinade on both sides.

- Preheat the grill to medium heat (350° to 450°F) for direct cooking. Preheat the grill for ten minutes with a griddle and/or large cast-iron skillet in the center.

- Put the salmon right on the griddle (hot) with flesh-side down first, using a metal spatula to evenly space the fillets, so they are convenient to flip. Shut the cap and sear the salmon fillets on direct heat, covered, for about 3 minutes, or until they can be lifted off the griddle. Toss the salmon fillets in the sauce and turn them over. Shut the lid and cook until the meat is done to your liking, about three to five minutes more for moderate rare, based on thickness.

2.5 Garlic Butter Salmon

Preparation time

25 minutes

Servings

4 persons

Ingredients

We have listed below the ingredients that would be required by you for cooking the healthy and tasty meal:

- 1 tablespoon finely minced fresh rosemary
- 1 teaspoon coarse sea salt
- 1/2 teaspoon pepper
- 4 salmon filets 6 ounces each
- 1 tablespoon minced garlic about 2 cloves
- 1/2 lemon juiced (about 1 tablespoon)

Instructions

Given below are the detailed instructions for cooking this tasty meal. You need to follow these instructions in the given order.

- Preheat the grill. Next, liberally spray a grill pan.
- Mix the rosemary, garlic, lemon juice, salt and pepper in a small bowl or mortar and pestle.
- Use all of the garlic paste to coat each piece of salmon.
- Remove the salmon from the refrigerator and spray it four times.

- Spray the bottom of each piece of salmon and flip it over, so the skin side is up on the grill pan.

- Cover and cook for 4-5 minutes before flipping each salmon filet.

- Remove the salmon from the grill when it is fully cooked and serve.

2.6 Cajun Garlic Butter Lobster Tails

Preparation time

20 minutes

Servings

4 persons

Ingredients

We have listed below the ingredients that would be required by you for cooking the healthy and tasty meal:

- 1/4 cup butter melted
- 1 Tablespoon olive oil
- 3 garlic cloves minced
- 4 lobster tails
- salt and pepper
- 1 Tablespoon Cajun Seasoning

Instructions

Given below are the detailed instructions for cooking this tasty meal. You need to follow these instructions in the given order.

- Heat the grill to medium-high. Begin by getting the lobster ready. Butterfly the tail by slicing down the center with kitchen shears. Pull the lobster meat upward by loosening the meat. Season the meat with salt and pepper and place it on a baking sheet.

- Mix olive oil, melted butter, garlic and Cajun seasoning in a small bowl. Brush on top of the lobster that has been prepared.

- Place lobster flesh side down on the grill for 3-4 minutes or until lightly charred. Cook for another 5 minutes on the other side, flipping it over and brushing it with the marinade again.

2.7 Grilled Halibut

Preparation time

25 minutes

Servings

4 persons

Ingredients

We have listed below the ingredients that would be required by you for cooking the healthy and tasty meal:

- Freshly ground black pepper

- Kosher salt

- Freshly ground black pepper

- 1 mango, diced

- 1 chopped red pepper

- 1/2 diced red onion

- 1 minced jalapeno

- 4 (4-6-oz.) halibut steaks

- 2 tbsp. extra-virgin olive oil

- 1 tbsp. cilantro, freshly chopped

- Kosher salt

- 1 lime Juice

Instructions

Given below are the detailed instructions for cooking this tasty meal. You need to follow these instructions in the given order.

- Preheat the grill to medium-high, as well as brush both sides of the halibut with oil before seasoning with salt and pepper.

- Then cook for five minutes per side on the grill until halibut is cooked through.

- In a medium mixing bowl, combine all ingredients as well as a season with salt and pepper. Serve the salsa alongside the halibut.

2.8 Maple Glazed Salmon Steaks

Preparation time

26 minutes

Servings

4 persons

Ingredients

We have listed below the ingredients that would be required by you for cooking the healthy and tasty meal:

- 1 cup diced grape tomatoes
- 4 salmon steaks, each about (6 ounces) and (1 inch) thick
- 1½ teaspoon
- ½ teaspoon freshly ground black pepper
- 2 scallions, sliced
- 1 tbsp. lemon juice
- 2 tbsp. Italian parsley leaves, chopped
- ½ tsp. cumin grounded
- virgin olive oil
- 2 ears corn, silk removed and shucked
- 1 poblano pepper, diced, seeded (1 cup)
- Half tsp. kosher salt
- A quarter tsp. hot sauce
- A quarter tsp. black pepper, freshly ground

Glaze:

- 2 tbsp. Dijon mustard

- 2 tbsp. maple syrup

- 1 tsp. fresh lime juice

- 1 tbsp. extra-virgin olive oil

- A quarter tsp. cumin, grounded

Instructions

Given below are the detailed instructions for cooking this tasty meal. You need to follow these instructions in the given order.

- Preheat the grill to moderate heat (350° - 450°F) for direct cooking.

- Brush the corn lightly with oil. With the lid shut, grill the corn on moderate flame.

- Put one tbsp. Olive oil, lime juice, cumin, hot sauce, mustard, salt & pepper in a small mixing bowl. Pour the mixture on the corn and mix well. While you're preparing the salmon, keep it refrigerated.

- Preheat the grill to moderate flame (400° - 500°F) for direct cooking.

- All the glaze materials should be whisked together in a small bowl.

- Season both sides of the salmon steaks with salt & black pepper. Brush the salmon with the glaze and place it on the grill at the direct moderate flame. Cook the salmon are basting twice for 8 to 10 minutes, with the lid shut, until the steaks can be lifted off the cooking grilles. Cook till a thermometer is placed into the thick portion of the salmon records 125° - 130°F, then flip the steaks and brush with the glaze.

- Serve the salmon steaks with the salsa while they're still warm.

2.9 Lemony Grilled Salmon

Preparation time

30 minutes

Servings

4 persons

Ingredients

We have listed below the ingredients that would be required by you for cooking the healthy and tasty meal:

- kosher salt

- Freshly ground black pepper

- Two lemons, sliced

- 4 6-oz. skin-on salmon fillets

- Extra-virgin olive oil for brushing

- 2 tbsp. butter

Instructions

Given below are the detailed instructions for cooking this tasty meal. You need to follow these instructions in the given order.

- Preheat the grill to high heat. Season the salmon with pepper and salt after brushing it with oil. Grill the salmon and lemon slices for 5 minutes per side, or until the salmon is cooked through and the lemons are charred.

- Top the salmon with a pat of butter and grilled lemons as soon as it comes off the grill. Serve and have fun.

2.10 Grilled Shrimp Tacos with Sriracha Slaw

Preparation time

40 minutes

Servings

4 persons

Ingredients

We have listed below the ingredients that would be required by you for cooking the healthy and tasty meal:

- A quarter cup extra-virgin olive oil

- kosher salt

- Freshly ground black pepper

- 1 lb. large shrimp, peeled and deveined

- 1/4 head red cabbage, shredded

- A quarter cup of mayonnaise

- 1 tbsp sriracha

- 3 tbsp. cilantro, freshly chopped

- 3 limes Juice

- 4 medium tortillas

Instructions

Given below are the detailed instructions for cooking this tasty meal. You need to follow these instructions in the given order.

- Combine olive oil, cilantro and one-third of the lime juice in a small bowl. Add salt and pepper to taste.

- Pour the mixture over the shrimp in a baking dish. Toss until everything is evenly coated, then set aside for 20 minutes to marinate.

- Meanwhile, prepare the slaw: Stir cabbage with mayo, remaining lime juice, and Sriracha in a large mixing bowl.

- Then season with salt and pepper as per taste

- Preheat the grill to high heat. Then cook 3 minutes per side, skewer shrimp and grill until charred.

- Then grill one minute per side on the grill until tortillas are charred.

- Serve the shrimp with slaw in tortillas.

2.11 Grilled Tilapia

Preparation time

20 minutes

Servings

3 persons

Ingredients

We have listed below the ingredients that would be required by you for cooking the healthy and tasty meal:

- 1/4 small red onion, thinly sliced

- 3 (8-oz.) tilapia filets

- 1/2 c. grape tomatoes

- 2 tbsp. fresh oregano leaves

- Kosher salt

- 3 tbsp. extra-virgin olive oil, divided

- 2 tbsp. red wine vinegar

- Freshly ground black pepper

Instructions

Given below are the detailed instructions for cooking this tasty meal. You need to follow these instructions in the given order.

- Heat the grill to medium-high.

- Then put two tablespoons olive oil + 2 tablespoons red wine vinegar in a medium mixing bowl. Season with salt and pepper after adding the red onion and oregano

- In this step, you have to season tilapia with salt and pepper after brushing with the remaining olive oil. Place the fillets as well as grape tomatoes on a grill that has been preheated. Cook grape tomatoes for about 4 minutes, or until soft and blistered. Grill tilapia for 4 minutes per side, or until the edges are opaque, as well as the flesh, easily slides off the grill.

- Transfer the fish to a serving plate. Toss the grilled tomatoes with the vinegar mixture and serve it over the fillets. Serve right away.

2.12 Grilled Branzino

Preparation time

30 minutes

Servings

2 persons

Ingredients

We have listed below the ingredients that would be required by you for cooking the healthy and tasty meal:

- 1/2 teaspoon pepper
- 1/2 cup olive oil
- cracked pepper
- optional chili flakes
- 1 lemon
- a handful of herbs- thyme, sage, rosemary, or parsley
- 1 bunch finely chopped parsley (tender stems, 1 cup)
- 1 whole branzino- gutted, cleaned, descaled (1.25- 2lbs)
- 1 tbsp. olive oil
- Quarter cup preserved lemons, chopped (flesh and rind)
- 1 tsp. sea salt
- 2 finely chopped garlic cloves

Instructions

Given below are the detailed instructions for cooking this tasty meal. You need to follow these instructions in the given order.

- Season the fish both out and inside with salt & pepper.

- Cut few lemons and stuff them into the fish's cavity. Add fresh herbs like rosemary, sage, thyme, or parsley.

- Cut two to three slits on each side of the thick end of the fish with a sharp knife. Because the end of the tail cooks faster as compared to the head end, the grill will cook more evenly.

  1. Preheat the grill to 400 degrees Fahrenheit, as well as oil the grates. Reduce the heat on one side if possible.

- Put the fish on an oiled grill with the end of the tail facing down. Grill a one and a half-pound fish for about five minutes, covered, without moving it, or until grill marks appear.

- To flip the pancakes, use tongs and a metal spatula. Cover and grill for another 4-5 minutes, or till crisp with conspicuous eyes cloud and grill marks.

- End up making the tasty Preserved Lemon Gremolata as the fish is grilling by combining all the ingredients in a mixing bowl and stirring well.

- Serve with a leafy green salad and Everyday Quinoa.

2.13 Cajun Grilled Shrimp

Preparation time

30 minutes

Servings

3 persons

Ingredients

We have listed below the ingredients that would be required by you for cooking the healthy and tasty meal:

- 3 garlic cloves, minced
- 2 pounds uncooked medium shrimp, peeled and deveined with tails on
- 4 medium lemons, each cut into 8 wedges
- 2 teaspoons paprika
- 1 teaspoon salt
- 1/4 teaspoon pepper
- 3 green onions, finely chopped
- 2 tablespoons lemon juice
- 1 tablespoon olive oil
- 1/4 teaspoon cayenne pepper

Instructions

Given below are the detailed instructions for cooking this tasty meal. You need to follow these instructions in the given order.

- Mix the first eight ingredients in a large shallow dish. Toss in the shrimp as well as turn to coat. Refrigerate for fifteen minutes after covering.

- Drain the shrimp and toss out the marinade. Thread shrimp and lemon wedges onto twelve metal or soaked wooden skewers.

- Turn after six to eight minutes, cover, over medium heat or 4 inches from the heat, till shrimp turn pink, turning once.

2.14 Grilled Lobster Tail

Preparation time

25 minutes

Servings

4 persons

Ingredients

We have listed below the ingredients that would be required by you for cooking the healthy and tasty meal:

- 2 tablespoon chives, freshly chopped for garnish
- Extra-virgin olive oil for brushing
- Freshly ground black pepper
- Pinch of crushed red pepper flakes
- 2 tablespoon parsley, freshly chopped for garnish
- 1 minced clove garlic
- ¼ teaspoon kosher salt, for seasoning
- 4 (8 ounces) lobster tails
- 1/4 c. melted butter
- 1 tbsp. lemon juice
- 1/2 tsp. lemon zest
- Lemon slices, for serving

Instructions

Given below are the detailed instructions for cooking this tasty meal. You need to follow these instructions in the given order.

- Preheat a grill pan or a grill over medium-high heat. Stir together parsley, lemon juice, melted butter, zest, garlic, chives, and salt in a small bowl.

- Cut the top of the lobster shell from the meaty part of the tail with kitchen shears. Cut in half the meat from the center with a knife. To keep the lobster from twisting while cooking, insert a skewer lengthwise through it.

- Season with salt & pepper after brushing with oil. Grill for 6 minutes, flesh side down, till evenly charred. Add a spoonful of the butter mixture on the flesh side of the lobster. Cook for five more minutes more on the grill until cooked completely.

- Remove the lobster from the grill and season with a pinch of red pepper flakes. Serve along with slices of lemon on the side.

2.15 Cedar Planked Salmon with Lemon Butter

Preparation time

50 minutes

Servings

4 persons

Ingredients

We have listed below the ingredients that would be required by you for cooking the healthy and tasty meal:

- A half teaspoon kosher salt
- 1 middle-cut salmon fillet, skin-on, (3/4" to 1¼") thick, bones removed
- 1 lemon, thinly sliced, seeded
- ¼ tsp. black pepper, freshly ground
- 2 tbsp. olive oil
- 2 tsp. brown sugar
- 4 tablespoons unsalted butter, softened
- 1 tsp. dill, finely chopped
- 1 tsp. kosher salt
- A half teaspoon finely grated lemon zest
- 1 tsp. lemon zest, finely grated
- A half teaspoon freshly ground black pepper

Instructions

Given below are the detailed instructions for cooking this tasty meal. You need to follow these instructions in the given order.

- In a shallow mixing cup, combine all the butter ingredients and mix well with a spoon.

- Soak the cedar plank in a baking dish full of water. Soak for one hour after filling it down with cans.

- Combine all the oil ingredients in a shallow bowl.

- Put the salmon on the shelf, skin side down. Cut the salmon into four serving sections without piercing the flesh. Brush about 1/3 of the oil onto the salmon flesh.

- Preheat the grill to moderate flame (400° - 500°F) for cooking.

- Cover the lid and position the plank over direct heat. After up to 3 minutes, use tongs to flip the plank over as it starts to smoke and toast. Place the salmon skin-side down on the plank's toasted side. Place the lemon slices on top of the salmon and spray them gently with the remaining oil.

- With the closed lid, grill the salmon over direct low heat before a thermometer placed into the thickest section of the salmon reaches 125° - 130°F.

- Switch the fillet on the plank to a heat-proof surface before serving. Remove the skins from the portions and serve with the limes and lemon butter sheets.

2.16 Grilled Fish Tacos with Creamy Chipotle Sauce

Preparation time

30 minutes

Servings

8-10 persons

Ingredients

We have listed below the ingredients that would be required by you for cooking the healthy and tasty meal:

- 1/4 tsp. ground cumin
- 1 small white onion, minced
- 1 medium tomato, cored and finely chopped
- 2 limes, cut into wedges
- 1/4 tsp. dried dill
- 1 canned chipotle chile in adobo sauce, plus 1 tsp. sauce
- Kosher salt, to taste
- 1 tsp. garlic powder
- 1 tsp. paprika
- A half tsp. cayenne
- A half-cup mayonnaise
- 1/3 cup plain whole-milk Greek yogurt
- A half tsp. dried Mexican oregano
- A half tsp. ground cumin
- A half tsp. dried Mexican oregano

- 2 1/2 lb. skinless, boneless tilapia fillets, cut in half lengthwise

- Kosher salt, to taste

- Canola oil for grilling

- 8" flour tortillas corn, warmed

- ¼ small cabbage, very thinly shredded

Instructions

Given below are the detailed instructions for cooking this tasty meal. You need to follow these instructions in the given order.

- To make the sauce, puree all of the ingredients together in a blender or food processor until smooth. Keep it refrigerated until you're ready to use it.

- In a charcoal grill, build a medium-hot fire, or heat a gas grill to high. Combine paprika, garlic powder, cayenne, cumin, and oregano in a small bowl; set aside. Refrigerate the fish for 15 minutes after patting it dry, seasoning it with salt and spices. Working in batches if necessary, brush the grill or skillet with oil and cook the fish, flipping once, till cooked through about 5 minutes.

- Serve grilled fish with cabbage, onion, tomato, as well as a drizzle of chipotle sauce, if desired, on warm tortillas with a squeeze of lime.

2.17 Grilled Oysters with Pecorino and Shaved Bottarga

Preparation time

30 minutes

Servings

8-10 persons

Ingredients

We have listed below the ingredients that would be required by you for cooking the healthy and tasty meal:

- 1 1/2 tsp. minced garlic
- 2 dozen oysters, such as Gulf or blue point
- Mullet bottarga and Aged Pecorino Romano
- 1 ½ tsp. minced thyme leaves
- Kosher salt and freshly ground black pepper
- 2 sticks unsalted butter, softened
- 2 tbsp. fresh lemon juice

Instructions

Given below are the detailed instructions for cooking this tasty meal. You need to follow these instructions in the given order.

- Preheat the grill. Season the butter, garlic, lemon juice and thyme with salt and pepper in a large mixing bowl. Shuck the oysters, leaving the meat as well as juices in the concave shell, and top each with a teaspoon of the compound butter.

- Place the oyster halves on the grill, shell side down, and cook for about 5 minutes, or till the juices begin to bubble as well as the oyster meat just begins to curl at the edges. Transfer the oysters to a serving platter after removing them from the grill.

2.18 Grilled Foil Packets Caesar Salmon

Preparation time

25 minutes

Servings

2 persons

Ingredients

We have listed below the ingredients that would be required by you for cooking the healthy and tasty meal:

- Two tablespoons creamy Caesar dressing
- 2 lemons sliced
- 2 tomatoes cut in wedges
- 6 sliced sweet peppers
- salt and pepper
- 6 grilled and jarred artichoke hearts
- 1 tbsp. fresh lime juice
- 2 sheets Reynolds Wrap foil
- 2 6-ounce Salmon Filets
- 1 tbsp. olive oil

Instructions

Given below are the detailed instructions for cooking this tasty meal. You need to follow these instructions in the given order.

- Preheat the grill to 450 degrees Fahrenheit.

- Fold both sheets of foil in half on a tray, leaving one side open.

- On the side of each sheet of foil, put the salmon in the center.

- Vegetables should be placed around every slice of salmon.

- Season to taste with salt & pepper.

- To each salmon filet, squeeze half a tbsp of fresh lime juice.

- Drizzle ½ tbsp. Olive oil over every salmon and vegan group.

- 1 tablespoon Caesar dressing, brushed on every salmon filet.

- Each salmon filet should have three lemon wedges on it.

- To make the foil packets, fold the topmost part of the foil as well as tighten up the edges.

- Place the salmon on the grill for fifteen minutes or until it is cooked fully.

2.19 Grilled Shrimp Foil Packets

Preparation time

25 minutes

Servings

4 persons

Ingredients

We have listed below the ingredients that would be required by you for cooking the healthy and tasty meal:

- 2 ears corn, cut into 4 pieces crosswise
- 2 tbsp. freshly chopped parsley
- 4 tbsp. butter
- 1 lemon, sliced into thin wedges
- 2 tablespoon olive oil
- 1-pound red bliss potatoes, cut into 1" pieces
- 1 ½ lb. large shrimp, peeled and deveined
- 2 cloves garlic, minced
- 2 smoked andouille sausages, thinly sliced
- Kosher salt
- 1 tablespoon Old Bay seasoning
- Black pepper, freshly ground

Instructions

Given below are the detailed instructions for cooking this tasty meal. You need to follow these instructions in the given order.

- Preheat the grill to high or the oven to 425°F. Cut four 12-inch-long pieces of foil. Over the foil sheets, evenly distribute the sausage, shrimp, garlic, corn and potatoes. Shower with oil, then season with Old Bay seasoning and salt and pepper to taste. To combine, gently toss everything together. Each mixture should be garnished with lemon, parsley, as well as butter.

- To completely cover the food, fold the foil packs crosswise on the boiled shrimp mixture. To seal the bottom and top edges, roll them together.

- Put foil packets on the grill as well as cook for 15 - 20 minutes, or until just cooked through.

2.20 Grilled Cedar Plank Salmon Burgers

Preparation time

30 minutes

Servings

4 persons

Ingredients

We have listed below the ingredients that would be required by you for cooking the healthy and tasty meal:

- Fillets of wild-caught salmon, weighing half a pound one and a half Avocado Mayonnaise (or mayo of choice)

- One and a half tbsp. Mustard that has been stone ground

- 1/2 red onion, diced

- 1 celery stalk, diced

- 2 tbsp Dill (fresh)

- 2 minced garlic cloves

- 2 tbsp. salt

- 1 tsp black pepper freshly squeezed lemon

Instructions

Given below are the detailed instructions for cooking this tasty meal. You need to follow these instructions in the given order.

- Prior to cooking, soak the cedar planks for about two hours. Preheat the grill to 350-375 degrees Fahrenheit.

- Cut off the skin as well as any bones from the salmon before dicing it into small chunks in the processor. Combine the avocado mayonnaise, salt, stone ground mustard, pepper, dill, and garlic in a mixing bowl. Pulse the salmon until it becomes paste-like and smooth.

- Place the salmon mix in a bowl after removing it from the processor. Mix in the red onion as well as celery until everything is well combined.

- Form four equivalent-sized patties, two for each plank. Grate the salmon for about 25 to 30 minutes or until it reaches the temperature of 145 degrees Fahrenheit.

- Serve the burger with the bun and toppings of your choice.

2.21 Easy Grilled Sesame Salmon

Preparation time

25 minutes

Servings

4 persons

Ingredients

We have listed below the ingredients that would be required by you for cooking the healthy and tasty meal:

- 1 tbsp. Toasted Sesame
- Salt & Pepper (to taste if needed)
- 2 tsp Olive Oil
- 1 tsp. Cumin
- 1 tsp. Coriander
- 1 Lemon, Zested
- 1/2 Salmon Filet
- 1/2 cup Pistachios, crushed

Instructions

Given below are the detailed instructions for cooking this tasty meal. You need to follow these instructions in the given order.

- Preheat your grill to 300 degrees F and prepare it for indirect heat.

- Over a baking sheet, put a greased cooling rack. Take out the salmon from the package, rinse if necessary, and pat dry thoroughly. If necessary, remove any pin bones.

- Pulse the pistachios in a food processor to make them finer.

- Combine all of the remaining ingredients, including the pistachios, in a mixing bowl and stir until well combined.

- Coat the salmon flesh lightly with olive oil, then apply a thin, even layer over the top.

- Cook the baking sheet indirectly on the cooler side of the grill till the thickest part attains 425 degrees F.

2.22 Easy Cedar Plank Salmon Salad

Preparation time

25 minutes

Servings

2 persons

Ingredients

We have listed below the ingredients that would be required by you for cooking the healthy and tasty meal:

- Salt & Pepper
- 1/2 Grilled Lemon, juiced
- 1/2-2/3 cup Avocado Mayo
- 1-2 tsp. Seasoning Salt or Old Bay
- 1/2 cup Celery, diced small
- 1/2 Red Onion, diced small
- 1/4 cup Capers
- 2 Salmon Fillets
- 2 tsp. Olive Oil
- 2 Stalks Fresh Dill, minced

Instructions

Given below are the detailed instructions for cooking this tasty meal. You need to follow these instructions in the given order.

- Preheat the grill to medium and prepare it for indirect cooking. 15 minutes before grilling, moisten the cedar planks in water.

- Put the salmon fillets on the planks, skin side down. Next season generously with salt and pepper after brushing the tops with a little olive oil

- On indirect heat, grill the salmon and lemon half till the internal temperature attains 145 degrees Fahrenheit (about 10-15 minutes). Remove it from the heat and set it aside to cool.

- Flake the salmon with a fork, leaving the skin on.

- Now season with salt along with lemon juice from the grill, and mayonnaise

- Serve in a low-carb tortilla.

2.23 Easy Grilled Sesame Shrimp with Shishito Peppers

Preparation time

20 minutes

Servings

8-12 persons

Ingredients

We have listed below the ingredients that would be required by you for cooking the healthy and tasty meal:

- 2 tbsp. Sesame Oil

- 1 teaspoon Salt and Pepper

- 1 to 2 tsp. Toasted Sesame Seeds

- 2 tbsp Chili Paste or Sauce

- 1 tbsp. Soy Sauce or Coconut Aminos

- 1 lb. Peeled & Deveined Shrimp

- 6 oz. Shishito Peppers

- 1 Lemon or Lime, juiced

Instructions

Given below are the detailed instructions for cooking this tasty meal. You need to follow these instructions in the given order.

- Set aside the shishito peppers with the remaining salt and pepper, sesame oil until you're ready to prepare the shrimp.

- Using skewers, skewer the peppers and shrimp. Thread each shrimp evenly onto both skewers, spacing them no more than an inch apart. It'll be easier to turn and grill as a result of this. Carry out the same procedure with your peppers.

- Heat the grill to moderately high and cook the shrimp and peppers for 1 or 2 minutes on each side. The shrimp is cooked to a temperature of 145 degrees Fahrenheit, as well as the peppers must have a little blistered skin all around.

- Remove the skewers and remove the meat from the grill. Serve with a dipping sauce and mix in a bowl with the toasted sesame seeds.

-

2.24 Scallop and Corn Bacon Burgers with Spicy Mayo

Preparation time

40 minutes

Servings

6 persons

Ingredients

We have listed below the ingredients that would be required by you for cooking the healthy and tasty meal:

- Kosher salt

- Pepper, freshly ground

- 6 lettuce leaves

- 12 slices cooked bacon

- 6 thick tomato slices

- 3 shucked ears corn

- 1 ½ lb. sea scallops (chopped)

- ½ cup mayonnaise

- Vegetable oil

- 3 tablespoons ketchup

- Tabasco sauce

- 6 hamburger buns (cut)

Instructions

Given below are the detailed instructions for cooking this tasty meal. You need to follow these instructions in the given order.

- Cook the corn in a pan of boiling water until soft for about 4 minutes. Place on a plate and set aside to cool slightly. Cut the kernels from the cobs while working over the plate.

- Put three-quarter cup corn kernels and ground to a paste in a food processor. To make a paste, combine 1/3 of the scallops, one and a half teaspoon salt, and half teaspoon pepper in a food mixer. Add the remainder scallops as well as a process until just combined; small chunks of scallop should remain in the mixture.

- Preheat the grill. Over moderate heat, cook the hamburger buns for 10 seconds. Coat the scallop burgers with oil as well as grill them over a medium-hot fire for about 4 minutes per side, or until nicely charred as well as just cooked from the center.

- On both halves of the buns, apply a layer of mayonnaise. Top with the scallop burgers and lettuce as well as tomato slices on the lower halves. Put two bacon slices on top of each burger Sandwiches should be served right away, with the remaining mayonnaise on edge.

2.25 Pop-Open Clams with Horseradish and Tabasco Sauce

Preparation time

15 minutes

Servings

4 persons

Ingredients

We have listed below the ingredients that would be required by you for cooking the healthy and tasty meal:

- 1/4 tsp. lemon zest, finely grated
- 2 dozen littleneck clams, scrubbed
- 1 tbsp. lemon juice
- Grilled slices of crusty white bread for serving
- 1/4 tsp. pimentón de la Vera sweet (Spanish paprika, smoked)
- 4 tablespoons unsalted butter, softened
- 2 tablespoons drained horseradish
- 1 tablespoon Tabasco
- Salt

Instructions

- Given below are the detailed instructions for cooking this tasty meal. You need to follow these instructions in the given order.

- Preheat the grill. Combine the butter, lemon zest, horseradish, Tabasco, lemon juice as well as pimentón de la Vera in a small bowl. Spice with salt and pepper.

- Grill the clams at high heat for about 25 seconds or till they pop up. Cautiously flip the clams so that the meaty side is down, using tongs. Cook for another 20 seconds, or until the clam extracts begin to simmer. Place the clams in a serving dish and set them aside. Serve with grilled bread and about ½ tsp. horseradish-Tabasco sauce on top of each clam.

2.26 Grilled Shellfish and Vegetables al Cartoccio

Preparation time

1 hour 10 minutes

Servings

4 persons

Ingredients

We have listed below the ingredients that would be required by you for cooking the healthy and tasty meal:

- Eight red radishes, stem attached, cut lengthwise
- 16 littleneck clams, scrubbed
- 24 large mussels, scrubbed
- 4 large basil sprigs
- 4 tomatoes, cut crosswise
- Olive oil
- 1 red onion, ½" wedges
- 1 bunch Broccoli
- Salt
- Eight fat asparagus spears
- Eight small carrots with some stem attached
- 16 little oysters, scrubbed like Wellfleet
- Warm crusty bread, for serving

Instructions

Given below are the detailed instructions for cooking this tasty meal. You need to follow these instructions in the given order.

- Preheat the grill. Mix all the vegetables in olive oil and salt in a large mixing bowl. Remove the broccoli from the oven and grill till lightly charred, approximately 1 minute each side, over moderately high heat. Place on a big plate.

- Then drizzle the olive oil over the clams, oysters, and mussels in 4 pairs of foil. Drizzle more olive oil over the vegetables and place them on top of the shellfish. Toss each with a basil sprig, a pinch of salt and 1 tbsp. of water. Roll the foil into rectangular packs by folding it tightly.

- Place the packs on the grill and arrange them as desired. Cover as well as cook at normal heat, tossing once or twice, for about 25 minutes, or until the packs are sizzled and puffed. Serve immediately with bread.

2.27 Grilled Shrimp with Shrimp Butter

Preparation time

30 minutes

Servings

6 persons

Ingredients

We have listed below the ingredients that would be required by you for cooking the recipe.

- 1 tsp. (belacan) Malaysian shrimp paste
- Black pepper
- 24 large shrimp, shelled and deveined
- 1 1/2 tsp. lime juice
- 6 tbsp. unsalted butter
- Half cup red onion, finely chopped
- 1 ½ tsp. red pepper, crushed
- Salt
- 6 wooden skewers, dripped for 30 mins in water

Instructions

Given below are the detailed instructions for cooking this tasty meal. You need to follow these instructions in the given order.

- Melt three tablespoons butter in a skillet. Cook, occasionally stirring, until the onion is softened, about 3 minutes. Cook, constantly stirring, for two minutes, until the red pepper, as well as shrimp paste, are fragrant.

- Then season with salt and lime juice as well as the remaining butter. Warm the butter with the shrimp.

- Preheat the grill or a grill saucepan. Salt and pepper the shrimp before threading them on the skewers. Grill for 4 minutes totals over high flame, flipping once, till lightly charred as well as just cooked completely. Shift to a serving platter and top with the shrimp butter. Serve garnished with mint leaves as well as sprouts.

2.28 Grilled Shrimp with Oregano and Lemon

Preparation time

1hour 30 minutes

Servings

8 persons

Ingredients

We have listed below the ingredients that would be required by you for cooking the healthy and tasty meal:

- 3/4 cup virgin olive oil
- Freshly ground pepper
- 2 ½ pounds large shrimp, shelled and deveined
- 1 tsp. lemon zest, finely grated
- 3 tbsp. lemon juice, freshly squeezed
- Half c. salted capers—soaked for one hour, rinsed and drained
- ½ c. oregano leaves
- 1 minced garlic clove
- Salt

Instructions

Given below are the detailed instructions for cooking this tasty meal. You need to follow these instructions in the given order.

- Finely chop the washed oregano leaves, capers, and garlic on a cutting board. Shift the mixture to a mixing bowl and add a half cup plus two tablespoons olive oil, as well as the lemon zest and juice. Flavor the sauce with a pinch of black pepper.

- Preheat the grill. Toss the shrimp with the remaining two tbsp of olive oil in a large mixing bowl and season gently with salt and pepper. Thread the shrimp on metal skewers as well as grill over high heat, flipping once, for 3 minutes per side, or until charred and cooked completely. Transfer the shrimp to a platter after removing them from the skewers. Serve with a dollop of sauce on top.

2.29 Grilled Sea Scallops with Corn Salad

Preparation time

1 hour 10 minutes

Servings

6 persons

Ingredients

We have listed below the ingredients that would be required by you for cooking the healthy and tasty meal:

- Salt and freshly ground pepper
- 1/4 cup plus 3 tablespoons safflower oil
- 1 1/2 pounds sea scallops (about 30)
- 1 small shallot, minced
- 2 tablespoons balsamic vinegar
- 2 tablespoons hot water
- 1/3 c. finely shredded basil leaves
- 1-pint halved grape tomatoes
- 3 scallions, light green and white parts only, sliced
- 1 teaspoon Dijon mustard

Instructions

Given below are the detailed instructions for cooking this tasty meal. You need to follow these instructions in the given order.

- Cook the corn until tender in a big pot of boiling water, about 5 minutes. Drain and set aside to cool. Remove the kernels from the corn and place them in a large bowl. Season with salt and pepper and add tomatoes, scallions, and basil.

- Puree the shallot along with the hot water, vinegar and mustard in a blender. Toss the corn salad with the vinaigrette, seasoning it with salt and pepper.

- Toss the scallops with the remaining one tbsp of oil in a large mixing bowl; season with salt and pepper. A large grill pan should be heated. Add half of the scallops to the pan at a time and cook, turning once, till browned, approximately 4 minutes per batch, over moderately high heat.

CHAPTER 3: Wood Pellet Grill Lamb Recipes

This chapter is dedicated to yummy lamb recipes that you will enjoy preparing on your wood pellet grill.

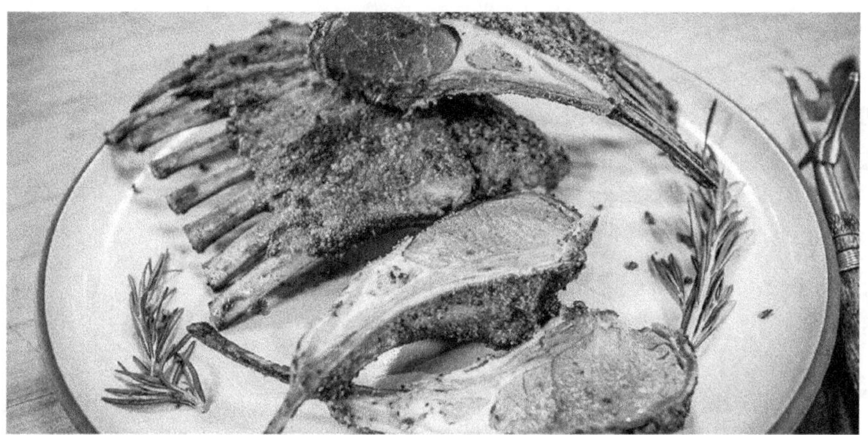

3.1 Rosemary Lamb Chops

Preparation time

32 minutes

Servings

4 persons

Ingredients

We have listed below the ingredients that would be required by you for cooking the healthy and tasty meal:

- 1 tbsp. fresh rosemary leaves, chopped
- Extra-virgin olive oil
- 2 pounds new potatoes, each about 1½ inches in diameter, quartered
- 2 tsp. thyme leaves, chopped
- 3 garlic cloves
- 1 teaspoon kosher salt
- ¾ tsp. black pepper, freshly ground
- 8 lamb loin chops, 1¼" thick and 4 oz., excess fat removed

Instructions

Given below are the detailed instructions for cooking this tasty meal. You need to follow these instructions in the given order.

- Garlic should be roughly chopped; then salt should be sprinkled on top.

- Preheat the grill to medium heat (350° to 450°F) for direct cooking.

- Brush both sides of the lamb chops with oil. Almost half of the spices mixture should be applied to both sides of the chops.

- In a medium mixing bowl, place the cut potatoes. Add 2 tbsp. Of oil on top and sprinkle with the remaining portion of the seasoning mix. Toss the potatoes to evenly coat them.

- Grill the potatoes for fifteen to twenty minutes, turning every five minutes, over direct medium heat with the lid closed. While you're grilling the lamb, remove it from the grill and keep it warm.

- Grate the lamb chops at direct moderate heat with the lid shut, turning once or twice, until done to your liking, for 8 minutes. Allow resting for three to five minutes after removing from the grill. With the potatoes, serve warm.

3.2 Grilled Herb Crusted Rack of Lamb

Preparation time

30 minutes

Servings

3 persons

Ingredients

We have listed below the ingredients that would be required by you for cooking the healthy and tasty meal:

- 2 teaspoons oregano chopped
- 1/4 teaspoon freshly ground black pepper
- 2 tablespoons olive oil
- 2 teaspoons mint chopped
- 1/2 teaspoon lemon zest
- 1 1/2 - 2-pound rack of lamb trimmed of excess fat
- 3 large cloves garlic minced
- 2 teaspoons rosemary chopped
- 1/2 teaspoon kosher salt

Instructions

Given below are the detailed instructions for cooking this tasty meal. You need to follow these instructions in the given order.

- To make the marinade, combine all of the ingredients in a small bowl to make a thick paste.

- Cover the lamb rack with the marinade. Refrigerate for eight hours or overnight, covered in plastic wrap.

- Preheat the grill to 500°-525° F. Then put the rack of lamb on the grill for 5 minutes to sear the meat.

- Reduce the temperature to 425°F. Turn the lamb over and roast for another 13-15 minutes, or until the temperature of the lamb attains 120° F for medium. Shift the lamb to a cutting board as well as cover with aluminum foil to keep it warm. Allow the lamb to rest for another 5-10 minutes.

- Make double-cut chops out of the lamb. Place the lamb on a platter as well as pour meat juices over it. Serve with a sprinkling of fresh herbs on top.

3.3 Racks of Lamb with Roasted-Shallot Vinaigrette

Preparation time

49 minutes

Servings

4 persons

Ingredients

We have listed below the ingredients that would be required by you for cooking the healthy and tasty meal:

- 1 teaspoon Dijon mustard
- 2 tablespoons finely chopped fresh thyme leaves
- ½ teaspoon kosher salt
- ½ teaspoon freshly ground black pepper
- 1 teaspoon finely chopped fresh thyme leaves
- ½ teaspoon kosher salt
- ¼ teaspoon freshly ground black pepper
- 1 large shallot, about 1 ounce, unpeeled
- ¼ cup extra-virgin olive oil, divided
- 1 tablespoon balsamic vinegar
- 2 lamb racks, each 1 to 1½ pounds, frenched
- Extra-virgin olive oil

Instructions

Given below are the detailed instructions for cooking this tasty meal. You need to follow these instructions in the given order.

- Preheat the grill to medium heat-350° to 450°F- for direct cooking.

- Brush a small amount of olive oil all over the shallot.

- Adjust the grill to medium heat-350° to 450°F- for indirect cooking.

- Brush the lamb with oil, as well as season with thyme, salt, and pepper evenly. To keep the bones from burning, cover them loosely with aluminum foil. Sear the lamb over direct heat, bone side down first, for two to four minutes, turning once, until lightly browned. Place the lamb at indirect medium heat, cover, and cook until done to your liking, about 15 minutes for medium-rare. Remove the chops from the grill and set them aside to rest for three to five minutes before slicing them into individual chops. With the vinaigrette, serve warm.

3.4 Grilled Lamb Chops

Preparation time

23 minutes

Servings

4 persons

Ingredients

We have listed below the ingredients that would be required by you for cooking the healthy and tasty meal:

- 1 cup olive oil

- 3/4 cup lemon juice

- 1 tablespoon chopped mint

- 1 tablespoon chopped Italian parsley

- 10-12 cloves garlic

- 1 teaspoon salt

- 1/4 teaspoon fresh ground black pepper

- 16 lamb chops

- 2 tablespoons avocado oil

- 2 tablespoons Greek Freak seasoning

- 1/4 teaspoon dry oregano

Instructions

Given below are the detailed instructions for cooking this tasty meal. You need to follow these instructions in the given order.

- Allow the lamb chops to marinate for 30 minutes in a baggie with one-fourth to one-third cup of the mint sauce.

- Remove the raw lamb from the marinade, as well as discard the remaining sauce.

- Heat the pellet grill to 450°F and season your lamb chops with Greek Freak seasoning before placing them on the grill.

- Cook for three to four minutes per side on each side, then set aside to rest.

3.5 Baby Lamb Chops Fire Roasted with Smoked Paprika-Orange BBQ Sauce

Preparation time

45 minutes

Servings

4-6 persons

Ingredients

We have listed below the ingredients that would be required by you for cooking the healthy and tasty meal:

- 1 cup fresh orange
- 1 tablespoon clover honey
- 1 tablespoon aged sherry vinegar
- 1 teaspoon finely grated orange zest
- 2 cups canned plum tomatoes pureed
- 1 tablespoon smoked paprika
- Half cup ketchup
- 1/2 tsp. coriander ground
- 2 tbsp. canola oil
- 2 cloves garlic, chopped
- 3 chopped shallots
- 2 tbsp. light brown sugar
- Kosher salt and black pepper, ground

- 12 baby lamb chops, with bone

Instructions

Given below are the detailed instructions for cooking this tasty meal. You need to follow these instructions in the given order.

- For direct grilling, preheat the grill to high. On both sides, brush the lamb with canola oil as well as a season with salt and pepper.

- Put the chops on the grill for 2 to 3 minutes on each side. Grill for another 2 to 3 minutes after flipping and brushing with some of the sauce. Transfer to a serving platter and top with the reserved sauce.

3.6 Lamb Chops Grilled in Rosemary Smoke

Preparation time

1hour 17 minutes

Servings

4 persons

Ingredients

We have listed below the ingredients that would be required by you for cooking the healthy and tasty meal:

- 8 garlic cloves, minced
- 8 large rosemary sprigs, stems with leaves (soaked in water at least 30 minutes)
- Rosemary sprig (for garnish)
- 2 teaspoons salt
- 1 teaspoon pepper
- 2 teaspoons olive oil (or more if needed)
- 12 lamb loin chops, trimmed of excess fat (at least 1 1/2 inches/4 cm thick)
- 1/4 cup chopped fresh rosemary leaf (or 2 Tb dried)

Instructions

Given below are the detailed instructions for cooking this tasty meal. You need to follow these instructions in the given order.

- Prepare the grill for high-heat direct cooking. Place the rosemary stems directly on the charcoal or gas burners. When the rosemary begins to smoke, place the chops over direct heat and cook, covered, for 3-6 minutes on each side, until done to your liking.

- Insert an instant thermometer away from the bone or cut into the chops near the bone to check for doneness. For medium-rare, take out the chops from the grill when the thermometer reads 130 degrees Fahrenheit (54 degrees Celsius), and the meat is still pink near the bone.

- Move the chops to a platter and set aside for 5 minutes, covered loosely with aluminum foil.

3.7 Steak burger with Tangy Caramelized Onions and Herb Butter

Preparation time

40 minutes

Servings

4 persons

Ingredients

We have listed below the ingredients that would be required by you for cooking the healthy and tasty meal:

- Kosher salt freshly ground black pepper
- 1 tbsp. parsley or tarragon, finely chopped
- 1 ½ lb. dry-aged steak, coarsely grounded
- 4 slices of cheddar cheese
- Green leaf lettuce or Romaine
- 2 tablespoons tomato paste
- 4 high-quality hamburger buns or brioche
- 3 tablespoons Worcestershire sauce
- 2 tablespoons white wine vinegar
- 2 tablespoons unsalted butter
- 1 tablespoon light brown sugar
- 2 tablespoons neutral vegetable oil, such as grape seed
- 2 medium onions, thinly sliced
- 1/2 teaspoon kosher salt
- 1/4 cup white wine vinegar

- 2 tablespoons finely chopped shallot (about 1 small shallot)

- 1/2 cup (1 stick) unsalted butter, room temperature

- Neutral vegetable oil, such as grapeseed (for the grill)

Instructions

Given below are the detailed instructions for cooking this tasty meal. You need to follow these instructions in the given order.

- To make the Tangy Caramelized Onions, combine all of the ingredients in a large mixing bowl.

- To make the herb butter, combine all of the ingredients in a small mixing bowl.

- Cut the ground steak into four equal portions. Form into 4-in. wide, 3/4-in. Thick patties that are loosely packed. To keep it flat as it grills, make a little dent in the center with your thumb.

- Oil the grates of a grill and heat it to medium-high. Season both sides of the patties with pepper and salt. Grill for 2–3 minutes, dented side down, till gently charred on the bottom. Give two to three more minutes for medium-rare. Toss, top with cheese as well as continue to grill until the desired doneness is reached.

- Meanwhile, toast the buns on the grill for about 30 seconds. If using, generously spread Herb Butter on the cut sides of the bun. Close the burgers by layering patty, lettuce, and three tablespoons caramelized onions on the bottom buns.

3.8 Grain Bowls with Grilled Steak, Corn, and Avocado

Preparation time

1 hr 10 minutes

Servings

4 persons

Ingredients

We have listed below the ingredients that would be required by you for cooking the healthy and tasty meal:

- 4 small or 3 large, shucked ears of corn
- 2 Tbsp. fresh lime juice
- 1 avocado, peeled, thinly sliced
- Creamy Jalapeño Sauce (for serving)
- 2 cups whole grains, cooked such as quinoa, rice, farro, or barley
- 3 ounces (½ cup) crumbled Cotija or feta cheese
- 1 pound flank steak or skirt
- 1 ½ tsp. kosher salt
- 1 tsp. black pepper, freshly ground
- 4 thinly sliced scallions
- ¼ cup olive oil

Instructions

Given below are the detailed instructions for cooking this tasty meal. You need to follow these instructions in the given order.

- Heat a grill pan at medium-high heat. Grill steak unless a thermometer inserted in the middle of the steak records 120 to 125°F. You should turn the steak occasionally. Move to a cutting board and set aside to cool for about 10 minutes.

- Meanwhile, char the corn on all sides on the grill for 10 minutes. Place on a cutting board and set aside to cool.

- Corn should be cut off the cobs and placed in a large mixing bowl. Stir in the lime juice, scallions, grains, feta, oil and half teaspoon salt. Divide the corn mixture between the bowls.

- Against the grain, thinly slice the steak. Serve the avocado and steak on top of the bowls.

- In the end, season with salt & pepper and drizzle along with jalapeno sauce.

3.9 Make-Ahead Instant Pot Grilled Ribs

Preparation time

2 hours

Servings

4 persons

Ingredients

We have listed below the ingredients that would be required by you for cooking the healthy and tasty meal:

- 2 Tbsp. brown sugar

- 2 Tbsp. red or white wine vinegar

- 2 garlic cloves, crushed

- 1/2 cup coarsely chopped parsley, dill, and/or mint leaves

- 1 Tbsp. kosher salt

- 1/2 tsp. ground cinnamon

- 4 lb. St. Louis–style pork spareribs, slice into 3 or 4-rib portions

- 1/4 cup dry white wine

- 1 Tbsp. black peppercorns

- 4 tsp. cumin seeds

- 1 1/2 tsp. crushed red pepper flakes

- Vegetable oil

Instructions

Given below are the detailed instructions for cooking this tasty meal. You need to follow these instructions in the given order.

- Preheat the grill to medium-high. Clean and lubricate the grate. Congealed fat should be spooned out of the cooking liquid, and the remaining liquid should be transferred to a small pot. Bring the mixture to a boil with vinegar and garlic.

- Cook occasionally swirling the pan until the liquid has been reduced by half, about 3 minutes. Strain into a glass measuring cup through a fine-mesh sieve.

- Rub a small amount of oil onto the ribs to lightly coat them. Grill the ribs for about 2 minutes or until they are lightly browned. Turn the ribs over, brush the sauce on the exposed side, and grill for another 2 minutes, or until the underside is lightly browned.

- Place the ribs on a cutting board and set them aside. Allow 5–10 minutes to cool before slicing into individual ribs. In the end, drizzle the remaining sauce on top, then top with herbs.

3.10 3-Ingredient Grilled Steak, Pineapple, and Avocado Salad

Preparation time

50 minutes

Servings

4-6 persons

Ingredients

We have listed below the ingredients that would be required by you for cooking the healthy and tasty meal:

- One teaspoon freshly ground black pepper, plus more
- 1 pineapple, peeled, cut into 1/2" rounds, center core removed, divided
- 2 pounds New York strip steak (about 3 [1"-thick] steaks)
- One and a half tsp kosher salt, divided, plus more
- 3 tablespoons olive oil, plus more for the grill
- 2 avocados

Instructions

Given below are the detailed instructions for cooking this tasty meal. You need to follow these instructions in the given order.

- Start by seasoning the steak with one tsp salt and one tsp pepper. Allow it to sit for at least 1 hour at room temperature.

- In a blender, puree one pineapple round, a half teaspoon salt, and 2 tablespoons water until smooth. Blend in 3 tbsp. Oil till smooth; set aside.

- Heat a grill to medium-high or a grill pan to medium-high; oil the grill grate or pan. 8–10 minutes for medium-rare, grill steaks as well as leftover pineapple rounds, occasionally turning, till the pineapple is lightly charred as well as an instant-read thermometer inserted in the middle of the steak registers 120°F.

- Place the steak on a cutting board and set it aside. Allow sitting for at least fifteen minutes before slicing thinly. To keep the pineapple warm, place it on a platter and cover it with foil.

- Cut avocados in half crosswise around the pit, then use your hands to carefully peel off the skin. Cut each half into 1/2" rings crosswise.

- Arrange sliced steak, avocado, and pineapple on a platter. Season with salt and pepper and drizzle with pineapple dressing.

3.11 Ultimate Grilled Lamb Burger

Preparation time

**20 minutes
Cook Time
30 minutes**
Servings

4 persons

Ingredients

We have listed below the ingredients that would be required by you for cooking the healthy and tasty meal:

BURGERS

- 1 minced and seeded Medium jalapeño pepper

- 2 Pound ground lamb

- 6 minced Medium scallions

- 2 Tablespoon fresh minced dill

- 2 Tablespoon fresh mint leaves

- kosher salt and black pepper

- 3 Clove garlic, minced

RED PEPPER MAYO

- 1/2 Teaspoon black pepper

- 1 Cup mayonnaise

- 1 Large red bell pepper

- 2 Teaspoon fresh lemon juice

- 1 Teaspoon kosher salt

- 2 Clove garlic

MAIN

- 4 Large brioche buns, halved, to serve

- 4 Slices manchego cheese

- 1 Cup baby arugula, to serve

- 1 thinly sliced Large ripe tomato, to serve

- 1 thinly sliced Medium red onion, to serve

Instructions

Given below are the detailed instructions for cooking this tasty meal. You need to follow these instructions in the given order.

- When you are ready to cook, preheat the Traeger to 500°F with the lid closed for 15 minutes.
- In a mixing bowl, combine the salt, lamb, scallions, jalapeno, mint, garlic, dill, and pepper. To combine, mix everything. Make 4 to 8 ounce patties out of the lamb mixture, approximately 3/4 inch thick. Set it aside.
- To make the red pepper mayo. Cook the red bell pepper for 20 minutes on a preheated Traeger, turning a quarter turn after every 5 minutes or until it has browned a little all over. Remove the peppers

from the grill and put them in a large resealable bag. Remove pepper from the bag after approximately 10 minutes, cut in half, peel off the skin and remove seeds.

- In a food processor, combine the mayonnaise, roasted red pepper, lemon juice, salt, garlic, and pepper and process until smooth. Set it aside
- Preheat the grill to 450°F or 500°F and cook the lamb burgers for 5 minutes each side for medium or until required doneness is achieved.
- Place your buns on the grill to toast for the last few minutes of cooking, then top burgers with a slice of cheese.
- Spread red pepper mayo on the toasted buns, place the burgers on top and top with onion, arugula, and tomato. Serve with a side dish of your choice. Have fun!

3.12 Smoked Lamb Sausage

Preparation time

120 minutes
Cook Time
60 minutes
Servings

6 persons

Ingredients

We have listed below the ingredients that would be required by you for cooking the healthy and tasty meal:

- 1 Tablespoon minced garlic
- 2 Pound lamb shoulders
- 1 Teaspoon cumin
- 1/2 Teaspoon cayenne pepper
- 1 Teaspoon paprika
- 2 Tablespoon ground Fennel
- 1 Tablespoon minced parsley
- 1 Tablespoon finely chopped cilantro
- 1 Teaspoon black pepper
- 1 hog casings
- 2 Tablespoon salt
- 3 Cup Greek yogurt
- 1 Clove garlic
- 1 Whole lemon juice
- 1 Tablespoon fresh or dried Dill
- 1 peeled Whole Cucumber,
- black pepper
- salt

Instructions

- Given below are the detailed instructions for cooking this tasty meal. You need to follow these instructions in the given order.
- Cut the lamb shoulder into 2" pieces and grind the meat in a meat grinder.
- Refrigerate the lamb after lightly combining it with all of the spices in a bowl. To give the sausage a proper texture, it's important to keep the ground lamb refrigerated, so the fat doesn't melt.
- Attach the hog casing (60 inches) to the sausage using a sausage horn, then feed the sausages through the grinder in order to fill the casing and then twist into links.
- Prick holes throughout the casing use a paring knife (which allows steam to escape while cooking). Then refrigerate.
- In a medium-sized mixing bowl, combine all of the ingredients for the yogurt sauce. Cover and put in the refrigerator.
- When ready to cook, preheat the Traeger to 225°F for 15 minutes with the lid closed.
- Smoke the sausage for 1 hour on the grill grate.
- Remove the links from the grill after an hour and preheat the grill to 500 degrees Fahrenheit.
- Place the links back on the grill after it has reached temperature and cook for 5 minutes on each side.
- Serve immediately with a serving of roasted potatoes and yogurt sauce. Have fun!

3.13 Roasted Leg of Lamb

Preparation time
30 minutes
Cook Time
60 minutes
Servings
8 persons
Ingredients

We have listed below the ingredients that would be required by you for cooking the healthy and tasty meal:

- 2 Teaspoon extra-virgin olive oil
- 1 (7-8 lb) bone-in leg of lamb
- 1 Tablespoon crushed garlic
- 4 Sprig rosemary, cut into 1 inch pieces
- 4 Clove garlic, sliced lengthwise
- 2 lemons
- black pepper
- salt

Instructions

Given below are the detailed instructions for cooking this tasty meal. You need to follow these instructions in the given order.

- Combine crushed garlic and olive oil in a mixing bowl. Rub the lamb leg with the mixture.
- Make approximately two dozen 3/4-inch, small, deep perforations in the lamb using a paring knife. Fill the perforations with slivered garlic and rosemary sprigs.
- Lemons should be zested and juiced, and the zest and juice should be uniformly distributed over the lamb. Season the lamb with salt and pepper before serving.

- Set the Traeger to 500°F and preheat for 15 minutes
  with the lid covered when you're ready to cook. Cook
  for 30 minutes on the grill with the leg of lamb.
- Reduce the grill temperature to 350°F and cook for 60
  to 90 minutes, or until the internal temperature
  reaches 130°F for medium-rare.
- Allow 15 minutes for the lamb to rest before carving.
  Have fun!

3.14 Hanging Leg of Lamb Gyros

Preparation time
60 minutes
Cook time
180 minutes
Servings
8-10 persons
Ingredients
We have listed below the ingredients that would be required by you for cooking the healthy and tasty meal:

- 4 OZ. cremini mushrooms
- 1 tablespoon black pepper
- ¼ cup dijon mustard
- 1 cup + 1 tablespoon divided grapeseed oil
- 8, smashed garlic cloves
- 5 LB, bone-in sirloin leg of lamb
- ½ tablespoon + 1 teaspoon dried, divided oregano
- ⅓ cup lemon juice
- 8-10 pita
- 1 tablespoon dried rosemary leaves
- Large wedge chop red onions
- ⅔ cup chopped scallions
- ½ tablespoon dried thyme
- 3 tablespoon coarse sea salt
- 1 chopped vine ripe tomato
- Tzatziki sauce

Instructions

- Given below are the detailed instructions for cooking this tasty meal. You need to follow these instructions in the given order.

- Preheat your Pit Boss Lockhart Grill to the "Smoke" setting. If you're going to use a gas or charcoal grill, make sure it's set to low, indirect heat.
- Combine grapeseed oil, mustard, lemon juice, scallions, rosemary, garlic, salt, thyme, and pepper in a food processor. Process until a thick marinade forms.
- The fat cap of the lamb should be scored, then trussed using butcher's string. Cover the leg of lamb completely with two-thirds of the marinade. Set aside the remaining marinade for the veggies. Wrap the lamb in foil and marinate for 1 hour at room temperature.
- Hang the truss from S hooks to hang the lamb in the smoking cabinet. Smoke for 45 minutes after inserting the temperature probe. Raise the temperature to 400 degrees Fahrenheit.
- Put the temperature in the top cabinet to 225 to 250°F (if using a grill or vertical smoker, set the temperature to 225°F). Once it reaches this temperature, completely open the upper chimney covers and reduce the grill temperature to 300°F. As long as the cabinet doors are closed, the temperature in the top cabinet should be maintained.
- Smoke the lamb for 3 hours or until the internal temperature reaches 135°F.
- While the lamb is cooking, skewer the red onion and mushrooms together on a skewer. Brush with the remaining marinade and cook for 3 to 5 minutes on the grill with the sear slide open. 1 tsp oregano, 1 tbsp grapeseed oil, While the skewers are on the grill, preheat the pita bread.
- Remove the leg of lamb from the smoker and wrap it in aluminum foil loosely. Allow 30 minutes for the meat to rest before slicing.

- Thinly slice the lamb and serve with chopped tomatoes, grilled onions and mushrooms, and tzatziki in a warm pita, if desired.

3.15 Chipotle Lamb

Preparation time
30 minutes
Cook time
120 minutes
Servings
6 persons
Ingredients

We have listed below the ingredients that would be required by you for cooking the healthy and tasty meal:

- 1 Tbsp chipotle peppers, crushed
- Black pepper
- 3/4 cup extra-virgin olive oil
- 2 Tbsp Italian parsley
- 2 Tbsp thyme, fresh sprigs
- 3 garlic, cloves
- ¼ cup applewood pit boss bacon rub
- 1 rack lamb ribs
- 2 Tbsp sage, fresh
- 2 Tbsp rosemary, fresh

Instructions

Given below are the detailed instructions for cooking this tasty meal. You need to follow these instructions in the given order.

Because lamb is a soft red meat, a lighter-smoking hardwood would be ideal like a Fruit Hardwood Pit Boss Blend.

- To make the dry rub, brush olive oil over the lamb ribs and season with black pepper and chipotle powder.

Refrigerate the lamb ribs for at least 15 minutes before serving.

- Preheat the Pit Boss Grill to 275 degrees Fahrenheit.
- Combine rosemary, thyme, Italian parsley, cilantro, sage, and oregano in a bowl with 1/4 cup Smoke Infused Pit Boss Applewood Bacon, 1/4 cup Extra Virgin Olive Oil, and 2-3 garlic cloves for the wet rub.
- Apply the wet rub to the lamb ribs all over.
- Place your bone-in lamb ribs on the grill and smoke them until they reach an internal temperature of 120-125°F.
- Raise the temperature of your grill to 425°F and sear until the temperature reached 135-145°F.
- Allow 10-15 minutes for rest. Carve and enjoy it!

3.16 Rosemary Citrus Grilled Lamb Chops

Preparation time
60 minutes
Cook time
15 minutes
Servings
4-6 persons
Ingredients
We have listed below the ingredients that would be required by you for cooking the healthy and tasty meal:

- 4 Finely minced garlic clove
- Juice from 1/2 lime
- 2 Tablespoons chophouse steak seasoning
- 2 Pounds thick cut lamb loin or rib chops
- Juice from 1/2 lemon
- ¼ Cup olive oil
- ¼ Cup red wine vinegar
- 3 Tablespoons orange juice

Instructions

Given below are the detailed instructions for cooking this tasty meal. You need to follow these instructions in the given order.

Lamb isn't only for Easter anymore! The lamb chops are a tasty and simple way to introduce your friends and family to a new protein. Garnish with rosemary springs for an additional special touch!

- Whisk together all of the ingredients, including 2 tablespoon Chophouse Steak, in a mixing bowl. In a glass baking pan, place the lamb chops and pour the marinade over them. To make sure the chops are fully coated, flip them over a few times.

- Allow the lamb chops to marinate for 4-12 hours in the glass pan covered with aluminum foil. Drain and discard the extra marinade after the meat has finished marinating.
- Preheat your Pit Boss to 400 degrees Fahrenheit. Set the grill to medium-high heat if you're using a gas or charcoal grill. Grill the chops for 5-7 minutes on each side on one side, then turn and grill for another 5-7 minutes on the other side at 350°F or medium heat.
- Before serving, remove the lamb chops from the grill, cover with foil, and set aside for 5 minutes.

3.17 Pistachio Crusted Roasted Lamb With Vegetables

Preparation time

20 minutes

Cook time

40 minutes

Servings

6 persons

Ingredients

We have listed below the ingredients that would be required by you for cooking the healthy and tasty meal:

- 2 Lamb, Racks
- Tablespoon vegetable oil
- 1 Teaspoon herbs de Provence
- black pepper
- salt
- 1 Bunch Peeled and Chopped Tri Color Carrots
- Tablespoon olive oil
- Pound fingerling potatoes
- 1/2 Teaspoon kosher salt
- 1 Clove minced garlic
- 1/2 Teaspoon ground black pepper
- 2 Teaspoon minced Thyme
- 2 Tablespoon breadcrumbs
- 2/3 Cup Chopped Pistachios
- 3 Tablespoon Dijon mustard
- 1 Tablespoon melted butter

Instructions

Given below are the detailed instructions for cooking this tasty meal. You need to follow these instructions in the given order.

- When ready to cook, increase the temperature to High and preheat for 15 minutes with the lid closed.
- Heat 1 tablespoon of vegetable oil in a large cast-iron pan on the grill. Allow for a 20-minute preheat time after closing the lid.
- Pat the lamb, dry it using some paper towels and season liberally with salt, herbs de Provence, and black pepper on each rack.
- Peel the carrots and cut them into 1" pieces in a large mixing bowl. Combine the olive oil, potatoes, salt, garlic, pepper, and thyme in a large mixing bowl. To combine, stir everything together.
- Brown the lamb on both sides in a pan for 6 to 8 minutes. Set aside the lamb in a baking pan, leaving the skillet on the grill.
- In a mixing bowl, combine pistachios, butter, bread crumbs, olive oil, and a sprinkle of salt and black pepper.
- On the fat side of each rack of the lamb, spread mustard. On top of the mustard, but the pistachio mixture.
- Directly on the grill grate next to the skillet, place racks of lamb. In the same skillet, add the seasoned carrots and potatoes. Cook for 15 minutes with the lid closed.
- After 15 minutes, remove the potatoes and carrots from the grill and stir them. Wrap the racks of lamb in foil and set them aside.
- Cook for another 5 to 10 minutes, or until an internal temperature of 125°F is reached when a thermometer is put diagonally into the thickest section of the meat.

- Remove the foil-wrapped lamb from the grill and set it aside to rest for 10 minutes. To test whether the potatoes are tender, poke them with a fork. If not, simmer for another 5 minutes or until the potatoes and carrots are cooked.
- Serve each rack of lamb cut into four double chops with roasted carrots and potatoes. Have fun!

3.18 Bbq Lamb Wraps

Preparation time
60 minutes
Cook time
120 minutes
Servings
4 persons
Ingredients

We have listed below the ingredients that would be required by you for cooking the healthy and tasty meal:

- 1 lemon, juiced
- 1 (2-1/2 to 3 lb) deboned leg of lamb
- olive oil
- 2 Cup Greek yogurt
- Traeger Big Game Rub
- 2 English cucumbers, cut into 1 inch cubes
- 2 Whole lemon zest
- 2 Clove garlic
- 2 juiced Whole lemons
- 2 Tablespoon fresh mint leaves
- 4 Tablespoon fresh chopped dill
- kosher salt
- 12 Pitas
- black pepper
- 3 diced Roma tomatoes
- 8 Ounce feta cheese
- 1 red sliced onion

Instructions

Given below are the detailed instructions for cooking this tasty meal. You need to follow these instructions in the given order.

- Allow the lamb to come to room temperature after removing it from the refrigerator.
- Rub the lemon juice and olive oil all over the outside of the lamb. Traeger Big Game rub is used to season the meat.
- Set the temperature to High and warm for 15 minutes with the lid covered when ready to cook.
- Preheat the oven to 350°F and roast the lamb for 30 minutes.
- Reduce the heat to 350°F and cook until the internal temperature of the thickest section of the meat - not touching the bone - reaches 140°F for medium-rare.
- While the lamb is roasting, whisk together all of the ingredients for the tzatziki sauce in a mixing dish. Place in the refrigerator to cool.
- Wrap the pitas in aluminum foil and place them on the grill to warm up for the final few minutes of cooking.
- Place the lamb on a cutting board and set it aside for 15 minutes before slicing it into thin slices on a diagonal.
- Fill a heated pita with red onion, lamb, diced tomato, tzatziki sauce, and feta crumble on top to make the wraps.
- Serve with fries and tzatziki on the side. Have fun!

3.19 Moroccan Ground Meat Kebabs

Preparation time
20 minutes
Cook time
30 minutes
Servings
2 persons
Ingredients
We have listed below the ingredients that would be required by you for cooking the healthy and tasty meal:

- 2/3 Cup minced onion

- 1 1/2 chilled Pound Ground Lamb or Ground Beef

- 2 Clove minced garlic

- 1 Tablespoon fresh mint

- 3 Tablespoon minced cilantro leaves

- 1 Tablespoon ground cumin

- 1 Teaspoon salt

- 1 Teaspoon paprika

- 1/2 Teaspoon ground coriander

- pita bread

- 1/4 Teaspoon ground cinnamon

Instructions

Given below are the detailed instructions for cooking this tasty meal. You need to follow these instructions in the given order.

- Combine all of the ingredients in a big mixing bowl, except the pita bread, in a large mixing bowl. Form into meatballs with a diameter of approximately 2 inches. Using a bamboo skewer, skewer each meatball, then soak your hands with cold water and shape the meat into a cigar shape approximately the size of a man's thumb. Refrigerate for at least 30 minutes, or even overnight, if possible. Preheat the oven to 350°F and leave the lid covered for 10 to 15 minutes when ready to cook.
- Grill the kebabs for 25 to 30 minutes, turning once, or until an instant-read meat thermometer reads 160 degrees within.
- If desired, warm the pita bread on the grill before serving.

3.20 Braised Lamb Shank

Preparation time
20 minutes
Cook time
4 Hours
Servings
4 persons
Ingredients

We have listed below the ingredients that would be required by you for cooking the healthy and tasty meal:

- Traeger Prime Rib Rub
- 4 Whole lamb shanks
- 1 Cup beef broth
- 4 Sprig fresh rosemary and thyme
- 1 Cup red wine

Instructions

Given below are the detailed instructions for cooking this tasty meal. You need to follow these instructions in the given order.

- Season the shanks with the the Rib Rub.
- When you are ready to cook, preheat the Traeger to 500°F with the lid closed for about 15 minutes.
- Cook the shanks directly on the grill grate for 20 minutes or until browned from the outside.
- Pour the beef broth, wine, and herbs over the shanks in a Dutch oven. Reduce the temperature to 325°F by covering with a tight-fitting lid and placing back on the grill grate.
- Cook the shanks for 3 to 4 hours, or until they reach an internal temperature of 180°F. If the tip of the

temperature probe comes into contact with bone, a false reading will occur.

- Carefully raise the cover and transfer the lamb to a tray or plate, along with any accumulated juices. Have fun!

3.21 Braised Lamb Shoulder Tacos

Preparation time
2 hours
Cook time
5 Hours
Servings
4 persons
Ingredients
We have listed below the ingredients that would be required by you for cooking the healthy and tasty meal:

- 1/4 Tablespoon coriander seeds
- 1/4 Tablespoon cumin seeds
- 1/4 Tablespoon pumpkin seeds
- 1 Tablespoon smoked paprika
- 2 Ounce guajillo peppers, seeded
- 1 Tablespoon lime juice
- 3 Clove garlic
- 1 Tablespoon fresh oregano
- 2 Tablespoon olive oil
- 3 Pound lamb shoulders
- 1 Tablespoon salt

Instructions

Given below are the detailed instructions for cooking this tasty meal. You need to follow these instructions in the given order.

- Finely grind the seeds with a spice grinder.
- Cover the guajillo chilies with water in a microwave-safe dish and microwave on high for 2 minutes. Allow it to cool slightly before transferring to a blender with two tablespoons of water. Garlic cloves, two

tablespoons olive oil, ground seeds, one tablespoon salt, paprika, oregano, lime juice, and two tablespoons olive oil Puree the sauce until it is completely smooth.

- Place the lamb in a medium roasting pan and massage 1/2 cup of the sauce all over it; set aside for at least 2 hours or more to 12 hours at room temperature.
- Preheat the Traeger to 325°F for 15 minutes with the lid closed when ready to cook.
- Fill the roasting pan halfway with water and cover it loosely with foil. Cook the lamb for 2-1/2 hours, occasionally adding water to the pan.
- Remove the foil and continue to simmer for another 2-1/2 hours, or until the lamb is brown and tender, spooning the juices on top regularly.
- After removing from the grill, set aside for 20 minutes. When the meat is cold enough to handle, shred it and mix it with the residual liquid in the pan's bottom.
- Serve with pickled radishes, sea salt, a squeeze of lime, and a sprig of cilantro on corn tortillas. Have fun!

3.22 Grilled Lamb Kebabs

Preparation time
15 minutes
Cook time
10 minutes
Servings
4 persons
Ingredients

We have listed below the ingredients that would be required by you for cooking the healthy and tasty meal:

- 1/2 Tablespoon salt
- 1/2 Cup olive oil
- 2 Teaspoon black pepper
- 1/2 Tablespoon finely chopped cilantro
- 2 Tablespoon fresh mint
- 3 Pound Boneless Leg of Lamb, cut into 2-inch cubes
- 1 Teaspoon cumin
- 1/2 Cup lemon juice
- 1 Tablespoon lemon zest
- 2 Whole red onion, cut into eighths
- 15 dried Whole Apricots

Instructions

Given below are the detailed instructions for cooking this tasty meal. You need to follow these instructions in the given order.

- Combine salt, mint, olive oil, pepper, zest, lemon juice, cumin, and cilantro in a medium mixing bowl and stir well. Toss in the lamb shoulder to coat. Refrigerate for at least one night to marinate.

- Remove the meat from the marinade and alternately thread the apricots, lamb, and red onion until the skewer is full.
- Preheat the oven to 400 degrees F and cook for 10-15 minutes with the lid covered.
- Place the skewers straight on the grill grate and then cook for 8-10 minutes (medium-rare) just until the onions are nicely browned, and the lamb is cooked to your liking.
- Remove off the grill and serve with your favorite sides, such as couscous, quinoa, or rice. Have fun!

3.23 Grilled Lamb Lollipops with Mango Chutney

Preparation time
15 minutes
Cook time
10 minutes
Servings
4 persons
Ingredients

We have listed below the ingredients that would be required by you for cooking the healthy and tasty meal:

- 1 Whole peeled, seeded and chopped Mango
- 6 frenched Whole Lamb Chops, around 3/4 thick
- 3 chopped Clove garlic
- 3 finely chopped Sprig cilantro
- 1/2 seeded and chopped Whole habanero pepper
- 1 Tablespoon lime juice
- 15 1/2 Teaspoon cracked black pepper
- 1 Teaspoon salt
- 2 Tablespoon chopped mint
- 1/2 Tablespoon coarse salt
- 2 Tablespoon olive oil

Instructions

Given below are the detailed instructions for cooking this tasty meal. You need to follow these instructions in the given order.

- If you can't get frenched lamb chops, cut and scrape the meat and fat off the bone using a sharp knife to make it seem like a lollipop.

- In a food processor, combine all chutney ingredients and pulse 15 times or till desired consistency is achieved; put aside. Mint should be chopped and set aside.
- When ready to cook, preheat the grill on high for 15 minutes with the lid covered.
- While the grill warms up, brush the lamb lollipops with olive oil on a baking sheet. Both sides should be coated. Season each side with salt and black pepper and set aside for 5 to 10 minutes at room temperature.
- Directly on the barbecue grate, place the lamb poppers. Close the cover and cook for 5 minutes on the grill. Turn the meat over and cook for another 3 minutes, or until an internal temperature of 130°F is reached using a thermometer put into the thickest area of the meat.
- Remove the steak from the grill and set it aside to rest for 10 minutes before serving.
- Sprinkle the fresh chopped mint over each lamb lollipop and spoon chutney on top. Have fun!

3.24 Smoked Lamb Leg with Salsa Verde

Preparation time
30 minutes
Cook time
3 hours
Servings
4 persons
Ingredients

We have listed below the ingredients that would be required by you for cooking the healthy and tasty meal:

- 2/3 Pound husked and washed tomatillos
- 4 Clove garlic
- 2/3 quartered Small yellow onion
- 2/3 Tablespoon drained capers
- 3 1/3 Whole serrano chile peppers
- 1/8 Cup finely chopped cilantro
- kosher salt
- 1/3 Teaspoon sugar
- 1 1/3 Tablespoon olive oil
- 2 Tablespoon fresh squeezed lime juice
- 2/3 Cup low sodium chicken broth
- 2/3 Fat Trimmed to 1/4" Thick, and Tied Whole Leg Of Aitchbone Removed, Lamb,
- 1 1/3 Tablespoon kosher salt
- 2/3 Head garlic, peeled
- 2/3 Teaspoon freshly ground black pepper
- 1 1/3 Tablespoon finely chopped Rosemary

Instructions

Given below are the detailed instructions for cooking this tasty meal. You need to follow these instructions in the given order.

- Preheat the oven to high for 15 minutes when you're ready to cook. Garlic should be threaded onto a skewer. Garlic, onion quarters, tomatillos, and chiles should all be grilled until dark brown spots appear on both sides, approximately 9 minutes for the onion, 6 minutes for the chilies and tomatillos, and 4 minutes for the garlic.
- Remove everything from the grill and immediately put the chiles in a ziplock bag. Allow 15 minutes for the chiles to steam in the bag. Preheat a cast-iron pan on the grill for 10 minutes with the lid closed.
- Remove the skin off the chilies and peel the garlic. Chop the chiles, onion, and garlic coarsely. Blend tomatillos, capers, and all other veggies together in a blender. 1/2 teaspoon sugar and cilantro Puree until completely smooth. Season with kosher salt to taste.
- In a hot cast iron pan, pour in the oil. Stir in the tomatillo mixture until it has slightly thickened, stirring often. 2 tablespoons lime juice and broth
- Allow mixture to reduce till it measures approximately 2-1/2 cups, then the close lid (about 15-20 minutes). Season the Verde with salt, sugar, and lime juice to taste. Allow cooling somewhat before covering and chilling. Remove the grill from the heat and reduce the temperature to 180°F.
- Dry the lamb and score the fat with the tip of a small sharp knife, making shallow cuts all over. Make small incisions all over the lamb with a paring knife and fill them with garlic cloves. Season the lamb with salt, pepper, and rosemary after rubbing it with olive oil.

Allow 30 minutes for the mixture to come to room temperature.

- Place the leg of lamb in the grill's center. Smoke the lamb for 30 minutes on the Smoke setting.
- Cook unless a thermometer placed into the thickest portion of the meat reads 130°F (approximately 1-1/2 hours) at 350°F.
- Allow it to rest for 15 to 25 minutes on a cutting board; the internal temperature should reach 140°F for medium-rare. Serve with salsa verde on the side. *Cook times may vary based on the temperature of the oven and the ambient temperature.

3.25 Lamb Stew

Preparation time
45 minutes
Cook time
1 hour
Servings
4 persons
Ingredients
We have listed below the ingredients that would be required by you for cooking the healthy and tasty meal:

- 2 Tablespoon olive oil
- salt and pepper
- 3 Pound Lamb, cut into 1/2" chunks
- 1/4 Cup tomato paste
- 4 Clove chopped garlic
- 2 Cup beef stock
- 2 Whole bay leaves
- 2 Tablespoon dried thyme
- 12 Ounce Stout Beer
- 1 Diced Large Turnip
- 3 Diced Large Carrot
- 2 Cup Diced onion
- mashed Potatoes
- 1 Large parsnips, peeled and diced into 1/2 inch pieces

Instructions

Given below are the detailed instructions for cooking this tasty meal. You need to follow these instructions in the given order.

- Preheat the oven to 450 degrees Fahrenheit with the lid covered when you're ready to cook (10-15 minutes).
- Season the lamb with salt and pepper before serving. In a Dutch Oven that has been preheated for 10-15 minutes, heat two tablespoons of oil.
- Cook the lamb pieces in the Dutch Oven one at a time, making sure they are well distributed and not overcrowded. Brown both sides of the lamb for 6-8 minutes before moving on to the next part, and so on until all of the lamb has been equally browned.
- Return all of the lambs to the Dutch Oven, along with the garlic, and cook for another 2 minutes. Cook for 1 minute after adding the tomato paste. Combine the beef stock, thyme, salt, beer, bay leaves, and pepper in a large mixing bowl. Preheat the oven to high.
- Brown the other veggies while the beef is frying. Cook for 1 hour or until veggies is soft. Serve with mashed potatoes on the side. Have fun!

3.26 Armenian Style Braised Lamb Shanks With Barley risotto

Preparation time

1 day

Cook time

8 hour

Servings

4 persons

Ingredients

We have listed below the ingredients that would be required by you for cooking the healthy and tasty meal:

- 1/4 Cup tomato paste
- 2 Tablespoon Pomegranate Molasses
- 1 Tablespoon garlic powder
- 1 Teaspoon Fenugreek
- 1 Tablespoon cinnamon
- 1 Teaspoon cumin
- 1 Teaspoon turmeric
- 1 Teaspoon cayenne pepper
- 1 Tablespoon salt
- 3 1/4 Quart Lamb Stock
- 4 Lamb Hind Shanks
- 2 Tablespoon olive oil
- 1 Cup Barley, pearl
- 1 Medium yellow onion
- 1/2 Cup Grated Parmigiano Reggiano

Instructions

Given below are the detailed instructions for cooking this tasty meal. You need to follow these instructions in the given order.

- Combine the tomato paste, pomegranate molasses, garlic powder, fenugreek, cinnamon, cumin, turmeric, cayenne, and one teaspoon of salt in a small mixing dish.
- Mix until the ingredients come together into a smooth paste. The spice paste may be prepared up to a week ahead of time. If you're making it ahead of time, keep it refrigerated.
- Remove the silver skin and big tendons from the lamb shanks before cooking. Refrigerate for at least 6 hours and up to 24 hours after evenly applying 1/4 of the spice paste on each shank.
- To prepare the lamb shanks, follow these instructions: Cover shanks halfway with lamb stock in a large cast-iron pan (or another oven-safe pan).
- When ready to cook, preheat the Traeger to 300°F for 15 minutes with the lid closed.
- Cook for 7–8 hours, flipping the shanks every hour. As required, add additional lamb stock to the skillet. When the flesh is soft and begins to come away from the bone, the shanks are ready.
- Start the barley risotto when the lamb is towards the end of its cooking time. One quart lamb or beef stock brought to a boil. Remove the pan from the heat and put it aside.
- Heat the olive oil in a medium saucepan and add the onions. Soften the onion in a skillet. Stir in the barley and toast for approximately two minutes. Add 1 cup of stock and two teaspoons of salt to the pot.
- Cook over low heat, stirring periodically until the barley has absorbed all of the liquid. Repeat this process, adding half a cup of stock at a time until the barley is fully cooked.
- Stir in the Parmigiano Reggiano and butter until well combined. Taste and season with salt if necessary.

- Serve the lamb with a risotto of barley. Have fun!

3.27 Grilled Butterflied Leg of Lamb

Preparation time
8 minutes
Cook time
40 minutes
Servings
8 persons
Ingredients
We have listed below the ingredients that would be required by you for cooking the healthy and tasty meal:

- 1/4 Cup red wine vinegar
- 1 Whole Lemons, Juiced and Rinds Reserved
- 4 Clove minced garlic
- 1 Teaspoon thyme
- 2 1/2 minced Teaspoon rosemary
- 1 Teaspoon salt
- 1 Cup olive oil
- 1 Teaspoon ground black pepper
- 1 Whole onion, sliced into rings
- 5 Pound butterflied (4-5 lb) leg of lamb, boneless

Instructions

Given below are the detailed instructions for cooking this tasty meal. You need to follow these instructions in the given order.

- To make the marinade, quarter the lemon and remove the seeds. Reserve the lemon rinds and squeeze the lemon juice into a mixing dish. Stir in the garlic, red wine vinegar, rosemary, salt, thyme, and pepper until the salt crystals have dissolved. Whisk in the olive oil.

- Remove the lamb's netting and put it in a big resealable plastic bag. Add the onion and the saved lemon rinds to the bag with the marinade. To evenly spread the marinade and herbs, massage the bag. Refrigerate for several hours or overnight in the refrigerator.
- Using paper towels, pat the lamb dry after removing it from the marinade. Remove the marinade.
- Preheat the oven to high for 15 minutes when you're ready to cook. Place the lamb fat-side down on the grill grate. For medium-rare, grill for 30-40 minutes on each side just until the internal temperature reaches 135°F. Allow 5 minutes for the lamb leg to rest before slicing. Slice thinly across the grain to serve. Have fun!

3.28 Braised Irish Lamb Stew

Preparation time
25 minutes
Cook time
2 hours
Servings
4 persons
Ingredients

We have listed below the ingredients that would be required by you for cooking the healthy and tasty meal:

- salt and pepper
- 4 Pound boneless lamb shoulder, cut into 1 inch pieces
- 2 Tablespoon extra-virgin olive oil
- 1 Large diced onion
- 8 Ounce chopped bacon
- 2 Clove minced garlic
- 4 Cup beef stock
- 1/2 Cup white wine
- 2 Whole bay leaves
- 1 Sprig fresh rosemary
- 2 Sprig fresh thyme
- 2 Large potatoes, peeled and diced into 1/2 inch pieces
- 1/4 Cup flour
- 2 Large carrots, peeled and cut into 1/2 inch pieces
- 1/4 Cup butter, at room temperature

Instructions

Given below are the detailed instructions for cooking this tasty meal. You need to follow these instructions in the given order.

- Set the Traeger to 350°F and preheat for 15 minutes with the lid covered when you're ready to cook.
- Season the lamb with salt and pepper before serving. In a Dutch oven, heat the olive oil over medium heat. Cook the lamb in batches and then put it aside.
- Cook, stirring periodically, for 15 to 20 minutes, or until bacon is lightly browned. With the exception of 2 tablespoons of bacon fat, remove the bacon and discard it.
- Return the fat to the Dutch oven, then add the onions and cook until they are translucent. Cook for another 30 seconds after adding the garlic. Return the lamb and bacon to the pan and deglaze with white wine; carefully remove all the browned pieces from the bottom of the pan with a wooden spoon.
- In a Dutch oven, combine the stock, herbs, potatoes, and carrots. Bring to a low boil, then reduce to low heat. Cover and cook on the grill. Allow for 1-1/2 to 2 hours of cook time, or until the lamb is soft and falling apart.
- Remove the stew from the grill and return it to medium heat on the stovetop. In a small bowl, combine the butter and flour, then mix into the stew. Allow cooling for 5 to 10 minutes, or until the stew coats the back of a spoon.
- To top, Season with salt and pepper. Remove the bay leaves and stems from the rosemary and thyme before serving. Have fun!

3.29 Slow Roasted Bbq Lamb Shoulder

Preparation time
20 minutes
Cook time
5 hours
Servings
4 persons
Ingredients

We have listed below the ingredients that would be required by you for cooking the healthy and tasty meal:

- 1/4 Teaspoon coriander seeds
- 1/4 Teaspoon caraway seeds
- 1/4 Teaspoon cumin seeds
- 2 Tablespoon water
- 2 Ounce dried ancho chiles, stemmed and seeded
- 1 Tablespoon smoked paprika
- 2 Clove garlic
- 1 Tablespoon lemon juice
- 2 Tablespoon extra-virgin olive oil
- 1 Teaspoon dried mint leaves
- 1 Tablespoon kosher salt
- MAIN
- naan bread, for serving
- 3 Pound bone-in lamb shoulder
- YOGURT SAUCE
- 1/4 Cup chopped cilantro
- 1/2 Cup Greek yogurt
- 2 Tablespoon olive oil
- 1 Clove garlic, mashed to a paste

Instructions

Given below are the detailed instructions for cooking this tasty meal. You need to follow these instructions in the given order.

- Finely grind the coriander, caraway, and cumin seeds in a spice grinder.
- Cover the ancho chiles with water in a microwave-safe dish and microwave on high for 2 minutes. Allow it to cool slightly before transferring to a blender with two tablespoons of water.
- Combine the paprika, ground spices, lemon juice, olive oil, garlic cloves, salt, and dried mint leaves in a large mixing bowl. Puree the harissa sauce until it is completely smooth.
- Place the lamb in a medium roasting pan and coat it with 1/2 cup harissa sauce. Allow sitting for at least 2 hours at room temperature.
- When ready to cook, preheat the Traeger to 325°F with the lid closed for 15 minutes.
- Fill the roasting pan halfway with water and cover it loosely with foil. Cook the lamb for 2-1/2 hours, occasionally adding water to the pan. Remove the foil and continue to cook for another 2-1/2 hours, or until the lamb is browned and tender, spooning pan juices on top regularly. Remove from the Traeger and set aside for 20 minutes.
- Meanwhile, mix the mashed garlic clove, cilantro, yogurt, and olive oil in a small bowl.
- Pull the lamb from the bone in big pieces using a fork. Pull the lamb into little shreds with your fingers and serve with the naan bread, yogurt sauce, and the leftover harissa sauce. Have fun!

3.30 Grilled Lamb Burgers with Pickled Onions

Preparation time
10 minutes
Cook time
10 minutes
Servings
4 persons
Ingredients

We have listed below the ingredients that would be required by you for cooking the healthy and tasty meal:

- 6 Tablespoon lime juice
- 1/2 red onion, thinly sliced
- 2 Teaspoon kosher salt
- 1 Cup Greek yogurt
- 1/2 Teaspoon raw cane sugar
- 2 Tablespoon lemon juice
- 2 Tablespoon Finely Chopped Herbs, like dill, mint, parsley
- 5 Clove minced garlic
- 1 Tablespoon olive oil
- 1 Pound ground lamb
- ½ finely diced red onion
- 8 Ounce ground pork
- 2 Tablespoon package fresh dill, chopped alongwith stems
- 3 Tablespoon fresh mint
- 3 Tablespoon minced parsley
- 1 Teaspoon ground coriander
- 1 1/2 Teaspoon ground cumin
- 1/2 Teaspoon freshly ground black pepper

- 1 sliced Tomatoes
- 6 buns
- butter lettuce
- Seedless Cucumber, Peeled and then Cut Into 1/2" Pieces

Instructions

Given below are the detailed instructions for cooking this tasty meal. You need to follow these instructions in the given order.

- Pickle the onions in a small bowl with the onion, lime juice, salt, and sugar. Stir to combine, cover, and set aside to soften for approximately 2 hours at room temperature. Keep it refrigerated until you're ready to use it.
- To prepare the Yogurt Sauce, combine all of the ingredients in a mixing bowl. Combine the yogurt, garlic, lemon juice, herbs, and 1/2 teaspoon salt in a small bowl. Season with salt to taste. Cover and chill for up to 2 days, or until ready to serve.
- Warm the olive oil in a small pan over medium heat to prepare the lamb burgers. Cook, turning regularly until the onion is softened, approximately 7 minutes. Allow cooling on a small platter.
- Combine the pork, lamb, mint, parsley, dill, garlic, coriander, pepper, cumin, salt, and cooled onions in a large mixing bowl. Using your hands, gently combine the ingredients. Make sure the meat isn't overworked.
- Make six equal balls out of the mixture. Form into patties and place on a baking sheet lined with parchment paper. If not used right away, cover and chill for up to 8 hours.
- Set the temperature to High and warm for 15 minutes with the lid covered when ready to cook.

- Place the burgers on the grill and cook for 2 to 3 minutes on each side for medium-rare, or 5 minutes on each side for well done.
- Before serving, place the burgers on a dish to rest for 5 minutes.
- Top burgers with a generous dollop of herbed yogurt sauce and some pickled onions on buns.
- If desired, sliced tomatoes, garnish with lettuce or cucumbers. Serve right away. Have fun!

CHAPTER 4: Wood Pellet Grill Beef Recipes

This chapter is dedicated to delicious beef recipes that you will enjoy preparing on your wood pellet grill.

4.1 Brisket

Preparation time

7 hours

Servings

6 persons

Ingredients

We have listed below the ingredients that would be required by you for cooking the healthy and tasty meal:

- ¼ cup paprika

- 2 tablespoons black pepper

- 2 tablespoons kosher salt

- 5-pound Brisket

- ¼ cup brown sugar

Instructions

Given below are the detailed instructions for cooking this tasty meal. You need to follow these instructions in the given order.

- Remove large chunks of fat as well as the fat cap from the brisket.

- Choose the rub you want to use.

- Apply a heavy rub of the spices to all sides of the brisket. It should then be refrigerated for a few hours or overnight after wrapping it in plastic wrap. Remove 1 hour before cooking from the refrigerator and set aside to rest at room temperature.

- Set up the grill while the brisket is resting. A constant temperature of 225°-250°F is ideal.

- Then over a drip pan, cook on the indirect side.

- Cook until the internal temperature reaches 200°-205° F.

- Wrap in foil and a couple of towels after removing them from the grill.

- Allow it to rest for one to two hours before serving by slicing thinly across the grain.

4.2 Sweet Tea Marinated Ribeyes

Preparation time

8 hours 30 minutes

Servings

4 persons

Ingredients

We have listed below the ingredients that would be required by you for cooking the healthy and tasty meal:

- 1 teaspoon black pepper
- A quarter cup lime juice
- 1 teaspoon salt
- 2 teaspoons sugar
- 1 teaspoon dried minced garlic
- 1 lime thinly sliced
- 3 sprigs of fresh rosemary
- 4 Ribeye Steaks
- 10 ounces grape or cherry tomatoes halved
- 4 cups Milo's Famous Sweet Tea
- A half tablespoon dried minced onion
- A half tablespoon dried minced garlic
- 1 tablespoon salt
- 10 ounces frozen corn cooked according to package instructions

- 12 ounces crumbled feta

- 15 ounces black beans drained and rinsed

- A quarter cup fresh cilantro chopped

Instructions

Given below are the detailed instructions for cooking this tasty meal. You need to follow these instructions in the given order.

- Whisk together the onion, salt, tea, garlic and pepper in a large mixing bowl. Insert the lime slices as well as rosemary sprigs in a large zip-lock bag.

- Put the ribeyes in the back and seal them properly.

- Refrigerate the bag for 2-8 hours.

- Remove the limes, liquid and rosemary from the fridge when ready to cook.

- Preheat the grill to 400 degrees Fahrenheit.

- Season each steak with pepper and salt on both sides.

- Cook for 8-10 minutes per side, or till the internal temperature attains 140-160 degrees Fahrenheit.

- Serve with Confetti Corn Salad on top.

- Combine the feta, black bean, tomatoes, corn and cilantro in a large mixing bowl. Whisk together the salt, lime juice, sugar and garlic in a separate small bowl.

- The sauce mixture is to be poured over the salad and coat it completely with a wooden spoon.

4.3 Hasselback Short Rib Bulgogi

Preparation time

3 hours 30 minutes

Servings

4 persons

Ingredients

We have listed below the ingredients that would be required by you for cooking the healthy and tasty meal:

- One tsp. sugar
- One tbsp. sesame oil, toasted
- 1.5 lb. 1"–1.5"-thick beef short ribs, boneless and trimmed
- Vegetable oil
- Kosher salt
- One tsp. sesame oil, toasted
- One tsp. sesame seeds, toasted
- 2 tsp. sesame oil, toasted
- 6 scallions
- 2 tsp. unseasoned rice vinegar
- One tsp. toasted seeds, sesame
- One 1-inch piece ginger, finely grated, peeled
- One tbsp. gochugaru
- One scallion, very finely chopped
- ¼ cup of soy sauce

- 2 grated garlic cloves

- ¼ cup white miso

- 2 Tbsp. dark or light brown sugar

- One tsp. gochujang (Korean hot pepper paste) or hot chili sauce (such as Sriracha)

- 2 Tbsp. rice vinegar, unseasoned

Instructions

Given below are the detailed instructions for cooking this tasty meal. You need to follow these instructions in the given order.

- In a small bowl, combine the sugar, miso, scallion, gochujang, oil, sesame seeds and one teaspoon of water.

- Scallions should be trimmed and cut in half lengthwise. Toss the scallions with the oil, vinegar, and sesame seeds in a medium mixing bowl.

- In a medium mixing bowl, combine the vinegar, ginger, garlic, gochugaru, soy sauce, brown sugar and sesame oil.

- Chop short ribs no more than halfway through the meat with a sharp knife. Turn the scallion over and cut the other side. Toss the meat with the marinade in the bowl, working the marinade into the slashes in the meat. Cover dish with a big plate and set aside for 2 hours or up to one day at room temperature.

- Set Up a grill for moderate-high heat with vegetable oil on the grate. Remove the short ribs from the marinade and season them lightly with salt. Turn every 1 to 2 minutes, and if necessary, move to a cold part of the grill.

- Transfer the short ribs to a shelf and set aside for at least five minutes before cutting through the slashes—or, to be honest, just ripping them apart.

- Season the scallion salad with salt and black pepper.

4.4 Grilled Steak Tacos

Preparation time

2hours 10 minutes

Servings

4 persons

Ingredients

We have listed below the ingredients that would be required by you for cooking the healthy and tasty meal:

- 1/2 tomato, chopped and seeded
- One teaspoon seafood seasoning
- One beef ribeye steak (1 pound), trimmed
- 8 flour tortillas (6 inches)
- 3 tbsp. ripe olives, sliced
- 2 tbsp. whole kernel corn, canned
- 2 tbsp. red sweet pepper, chopped
- 2 tbsp. lemon juice
- 4 tbsp. fresh cilantro, minced
- 1/4 cup mayonnaise
- 2 tsp. Sriracha chili sauce or 1 teaspoon hot pepper sauce
- 1/8 tsp. sesame oil
- One medium ripe avocado, peeled and finely chopped
- One tsp. onion, chopped
- 2 tsp. pepper

- One minced garlic clove

- 1/4 tsp. ground cumin

- One tsp. salt

- 2 tsp. olive oil

Instructions

Given below are the detailed instructions for cooking this tasty meal. You need to follow these instructions in the given order.

- Mix the aioli ingredients in a small bowl. Mix the salsa ingredients in a separate bowl. Refrigerate until ready to serve.

- Rub both sides of the steak with a mixture of pepper, oil, salt, and seafood seasoning.

- Cover and cook over medium heat until the meat is done to your liking; for medium-rare, a thermometer must read 135°F. Allow for a 5-minute rest period.

- In the meantime, warm tortillas on the grill for forty-five seconds on each side

- Place thinly sliced steak on tortillas. Serve it with salsa, aioli, and your favorite toppings.

4.5 California Burger Wraps

Preparation time

45 minutes

Servings

8 persons

Ingredients

We have listed below the ingredients that would be required by you for cooking the healthy and tasty meal:

- 8 Bibb lettuce leaves
- 1/2 medium ripe avocado, peeled and cut into 8 slices
- 1/4 cup chopped red onion
- 1/3 cup crumbled feta cheese
- 1 pound lean ground beef (90% lean)
- 1/2 teaspoon salt
- 1/4 teaspoon pepper
- 2 tablespoons Miracle Whip Light

Instructions

Given below are the detailed instructions for cooking this tasty meal. You need to follow these instructions in the given order.

- Combine beef, salt, and pepper in a large mixing bowl, stirring lightly but thoroughly. Form eight 1/2-inch-thick patties.

- Then the burgers are to be grilled for three to four minutes on each side at medium heat or broil 3-4 inches from heat till a thermometer reads 160°F. In lettuce leaves, place burgers. Spread feta as well as Miracle Whip on top of burgers.

4.6 Grilled Flank Steak

Preparation time

35 minutes

Servings

4 persons

Ingredients

We have listed below the ingredients that would be required by you for cooking the healthy and tasty meal:

- zest from one lime
- One tablespoon Gourmet Garden Stir-in Chunky Garlic Paste
- 1 tablespoon olive oil
- 2 lbs. Flank Steak
- 1 teaspoon finely chopped green onion
- 1 tablespoon Gourmet Garden Stir-In Chunky Garlic Paste
- 1 teaspoon salt
- 1/2 teaspoon black pepper
- 1/2 cup salted butter softened to room temperature
- One tablespoon Gourmet Garden Lightly Dried Cilantro
- 1 tablespoon fresh lime juice
- 1 teaspoon mustard powder

Instructions

Given below are the detailed instructions for cooking this tasty meal. You need to follow these instructions in the given order.

- Heat a grill or grill pan over high heat after brushing with canola oil.

- Combine salt, olive oil, pepper, garlic paste and mustard powder in a small bowl. To make a paste, combine all of the ingredients in a mixing bowl. Apply the paste to both sides of the steak.

- Grill flank steak for three to four minutes per side for rare, or six to eight minutes per side for well done.

- Remove the pan from the heat.

- Cut against the grain into slices.

- Slice the butter and place it on top of the steak for melting.

4.7 Jalapeño Popper Burgers

Preparation time

30 minutes

Servings

4 persons

Ingredients

We have listed below the ingredients that would be required by you for cooking the healthy and tasty meal:

- 2 jalapeños, minced
- 1/2 tsp. chili powder
- One and a half Angus ground beef
- Kosher salt
- Freshly ground black pepper
- 4 oz. cream cheese softened
- 1/2 c. shredded cheddar
- 1/2 c. shredded mozzarella
- 6 slices bacon, cooked and chopped
- Four burger buns

Instructions

Given below are the detailed instructions for cooking this tasty meal. You need to follow these instructions in the given order.

- Make eight large, thin rounds out of ground beef (approximately 14"). Fill one patty with about 14 cups of the filling mixture, then top with a second patty. Pinch the edges of the burger to seal it and, if necessary, reshape it into a disc. Repeat with the rest of the patties as well as a filling mixture.

- Preheat the grill to medium-high temperature. Salt, chili powder and pepper should be used on both sides of the burgers. Cook till cooked through to your liking on the grill, approximately 6 minutes per side for medium.

- Serve immediately with burger buns.

4.8 Steak Fajitas

Preparation time

2 hours 40 minutes

Servings

6 persons

Ingredients

We have listed below the ingredients that would be required by you for cooking the healthy and tasty meal:

- A half-cup canola oil
- One large green bell pepper stemmed, seeded and cut into 1/2 –inch-wide strips
- One large yellow or white onions cut
- Twelve pieces of 8-in corn tortillas warmed
- 3 tablespoons packed dark brown sugar
- 2 medium cloves garlic minced
- 2 medium jalapenos
- 1 tablespoon fajita seasoning
- 1 teaspoon ground cumin
- A half-cup low-sodium soy sauce
- Half-cup fresh lime juice 5-7 limes
- Juice from 1 large orange
- 1 teaspoon freshly ground black pepper
- Kosher salt to taste

- 2 pounds trimmed skirt steak cut with the grain into 5-inch pieces

- Three medium bell peppers, red, yellow & orange, stemmed, seeded and cut into 1/2 –inch-wide strips

Instructions

Given below are the detailed instructions for cooking this tasty meal. You need to follow these instructions in the given order.

- Mix fajita seasoning, orange juice, soy sauce, lime juice, jalapenos, canola oil, brown sugar, minced garlic, cumin, and black pepper in a medium mixing bowl.

- Place the cut steaks in a gallon-sized zip-lock bag with the marinade and seal the bag.

- Take out the meat from the fridge fifteen to thirty minutes before using it when ready to cook.

- Insert the cut vegetables into the reserved 12 cup marinade and toss to coat while the meat marinates. Refrigerate, occasionally stirring, until ready to use.

- Take the meat and vegetables out of the refrigerator.

- Wipe the surplus marinade from the meat with paper towels.

- Move the vegetables to the baking sheet with tongs, shaking off any excess marinade as you go.

- Cook for 4 minutes, then toss to redistribute the vegetables and cook for another 4-5 minutes, or till fork-tender as well as slightly charred.

- Preheat half of the burners to the highest setting, cover, and wait 10 minutes. Clean as well as oil the grate after 10 minutes.

- Put the meat on the hot side of the grill, cover, and cook for 6-8 minutes total, occasionally turning, until the steak has a beautiful char on both sides. An instant-read thermometer should read 125-130°F in the center of the meat.

- Drizzle any remaining meat juices as well as lime juice on top.

- Serve the meat and vegetables with warmed Mexican rice, salsa, chopped fresh cilantro, sour cream, tortillas, guacamole, Pico de Gallo, beans, cheese and lime wedges on a large serving platter.

4.9 Lacquered Rib Eye

Preparation time

1 hour 20 minutes

Servings

2-4 persons

Ingredients

We have listed below the ingredients that would be required by you for cooking the healthy and tasty meal:

- 2 tsp. sugar

- Flaky sea salt

- Lemon wedges (for serving)

- 1 garlic clove, crushed

- Vegetable oil (for the grill)

- 1 2–2½-lb. bone-in rib eye (about 2" thick),

- ¼ cup sherry vinegar or red wine vinegar

- 2 Tbsp. soy sauce

- 1 Tbsp. fish sauce

- Kosher salt

- Extra-virgin olive oil (for drizzling)

Instructions

Given below are the detailed instructions for cooking this tasty meal. You need to follow these instructions in the given order.

- In a small saucepan over medium-high heat, bring the sugar, garlic, vinegar, soy sauce and fish sauce to a simmer. Reduce heat to low and gently simmer till the liquid has been reduced by about half.

- Prepare a grill with a high-intensity indirect heat source.

- Cook the steak over indirect heat, turning every one to two minutes as well as moving closer to or farther away from the heat as needed to achieve even color, for 10–12 minutes, or till an instant-read thermometer placed in the thickest part of the steak registers 100°F. Begin basting the steak. Grill until the meat is very dark brown, and the thermometer reads 120°F for medium-rare.

- Slice the steak into thick strips on a cutting board. Arrange on a platter and drizzle with olive oil before seasoning with salt and pepper. Serve with lemon wedges on the side.

4.10 Classic burgers

Preparation time

20 minutes

Servings

3 persons

Ingredients

We have listed below the ingredients that would be required by you for cooking the healthy and tasty meal:

- Three slices of cheese, such as yellow cheddar
- Ketchup
- Mustard
- Mayonnaise
- 3 hamburger buns
- 1 large tomato, thinly sliced
- 1 lb. ground beef
- Kosher salt
- Freshly ground black pepper
- 1 small red onion, thinly sliced
- Three leaves butter or iceberg lettuce

Instructions

Given below are the detailed instructions for cooking this tasty meal. You need to follow these instructions in the given order.

- Form the beef into three equal-sized patties, each measuring about 3 1/2" in width. Season almost every patty generously with salt and pepper on both sides. Make a shallow indent in the middle of each burger with your finger.

- Preheat the grill to high heat. Patties should be grilled until a crust forms, and they are no longer pink, about six minutes per side for medium.

- Before serving, put patties on buns as well as top with desired toppings.

4.11 Pulled Beef Burritos

Preparation time

19 minutes

Servings

4 persons

Ingredients

We have listed below the ingredients that would be required by you for cooking the healthy and tasty meal:

- 1/4 cup light sour cream
- 1/2 cup shredded cheddar cheese
- 1/4 cup BBQ sauce
- 2 tablespoons fresh lime juice
- 1/4 cup fresh cilantro finely chopped
- 2 Large 12-inch flour tortillas
- 1 package Farm Rich Smokehouse Pulled Beef
- 2 cups white rice cooked
- 1 15 ounces can black beans, drained and rinsed

Instructions

Given below are the detailed instructions for cooking this tasty meal. You need to follow these instructions in the given order.

- Mix the lime juice, cilantro, rice and sour cream in a medium mixing bowl. Stir until everything is well combined and creamy. Remove from the equation.

- Half of the beef, rice, beans and cheese go into each tortilla. Roll it up like a burrito, bringing the sides in and tucking them in to seal it.

- Brush the tops of each burrito with a generous amount of BBQ sauce.

- Grill each burrito for five to seven minutes on each side over medium heat or until the tortilla is crisp and to your liking.

- Enjoy it with your friends.

4.12 Garlic and Red-Miso Porterhouse

Preparation time

3 hours 30 minutes

Servings

4 persons

Ingredients

We have listed below the ingredients that would be required by you for cooking the healthy and tasty meal:

- 3 tbsp. olive oil

- 8 cloves garlic, grated

- 1 (2") piece ginger, peeled and grated

- 3 tbsp. sesame oil

- ½ c. soy sauce

- 2 (1 1/2"-thick) porterhouse bone-in steaks (3 1/2 lb.)

- 1 tsp. black pepper, freshly ground

- ¼ c. red miso

Instructions

Given below are the detailed instructions for cooking this tasty meal. You need to follow these instructions in the given order.

- In a 9" x 13" baking dish, place the steaks. In a bowl, combine the oil, miso, garlic soy sauce, pepper and ginger; pour 34% of the marinade over the steaks. Set aside for ten minutes after covering with plastic wrap. Save the rest of the marinade.

- Preheat the grill to high heat. Grill steaks for 1 minute on the hot part of the grill without flipping.

- Move the steaks to the cold part of the grill and cook for 4 minutes, or until juices come on top of the steaks. Repeat the grilling process on the other side of the steaks. Return the steaks to the hottest portion of the grill and baste with the reserved marinade, brushing and flipping after few minutes till it is caramelized and the meat starts to fall away off the bone, ten to twelve minutes for moderate rare.

- Allow steaks to rest for 5 minutes before slicing against the grain with the bone. Serve and enjoy.

4.13 Florentine Steak

Preparation time

3 hours 30 minutes

Servings

4 persons

Ingredients

We have listed below the ingredients that would be required by you for cooking the healthy and tasty meal:

- Two (One and a half-inch thick) porterhouse steaks bone-in (3 1/2 lb.)
- A quarter cup olive oil
- Kosher salt
- Black pepper freshly ground to taste
- Lime wedges
- Two sprigs rosemary

Instructions

Given below are the detailed instructions for cooking this tasty meal. You need to follow these instructions in the given order.

- Preheat the wood pellet grill to high and brush half of the oil over the steaks before seasoning with salt and pepper.
- Grill for 4-6 minutes on the hottest part of the grill, flipping once, till browned. Brush the remaining oil over the steaks with rosemary sprigs.

- Cook until the desired doneness is reached, about 4-6 minutes longer for medium-rare or unless an instant-read thermometer registers 125°F. If the outside of the steak starts to burn before it's done, move it to the cooler side of the grill till it's done.

- Allow 5 minutes for the steaks to rest before slicing against the grain along the bone. Serve with lemon wedges on the side.

4.14 Angel Cruz Beef Skewers

Preparation time

3 hours 30 minutes

Servings

2-4 persons

Ingredients

We have listed below the ingredients that would be required by you for cooking the healthy and tasty meal:

- 2 shallots, finely chopped
- 1 (1-inch) piece ginger, peeled and minced
- 1 tsp. ground turmeric
- Six tbsp. oyster sauce
- 1 1/2 tbsp. sweet paprika
- 3 lb. beef chuck, cut into 1/2-inch pieces
- Six stalks lemongrass
- 6 kaffir lime leaves, finely chopped
- Six cloves garlic, peeled
- 1/2 cup plus 1 tbsp. honey
- 6 tbsp. vegetable oil
- Six tbsp. fish sauce

Instructions

Given below are the detailed instructions for cooking this tasty meal. You need to follow these instructions in the given order.

- Combine the lemongrass, turmeric, ginger, lime leaves, garlic and shallots in a food processor and pulse till smooth paste forms. In a large mixing bowl, combine the beef, oyster sauce, honey, fish sauce and paprika. Toss the beef in the sauce until it is evenly coated. Then cover with plastic wrap and chill for at least 3 hours.

- Preheat the grill. Thread the beef onto wooden skewers and grill, turning as needed, for about 8 minutes, or until charred and cooked through. Transfer to a serving platter and serve immediately.

4.15 Steak Sandwich Kabobs

Preparation time

25 minutes

Servings

4 persons

Ingredients

We have listed below the ingredients that would be required by you for cooking the healthy and tasty meal:

- 6 oz. focaccia bread, sliced into 1" cubes

- 2 cups deli coleslaw

- 1/2 cup chopped walnuts

- One medium onion, cut into 1" slices

- 1 tablespoon olive oil

- 1 lb. beef sirloin steak, sliced in 1" cubes

- 1 teaspoon steak seasoning

- One medium red sweet pepper, sliced into 1" pieces

- 3 slices provolone cheese, cut into strips

Instructions

Given below are the detailed instructions for cooking this tasty meal. You need to follow these instructions in the given order.

- Steak seasoning should be sprinkled over the beef. Thread the bread cubes, beef, red pepper and onion on 4 metal or soaked wooden skewers in alternate directions; brush with oil.

- Grill, covered, over medium heat for eight to ten minutes or until desired doneness is reached, turning once or twice. A thermometer must read 135°F for medium-rare, 140°F for medium, and 145°F for medium-well. Grill for an additional 1-2 minutes, or till cheese is melted.

- Combine the coleslaw and walnuts in a small mixing bowl. Serve alongside kabobs.

4.16 Tacos on a Stick

Preparation time

30 minutes

Servings

4 persons

Ingredients

We have listed below the ingredients that would be required by you for cooking the healthy and tasty meal:

- 2 pounds beef top sirloin steak, cut into 1-inch cubes
- 16 cherry tomatoes
- Salsa con queso or sour cream
- 1 medium green pepper, in chunks
- 1 medium sweet red pepper, in chunks
- 1 envelope taco seasoning
- 1 cup tomato juice
- 2 tablespoons canola oil
- 1 large onion, cut into wedges

Instructions

Given below are the detailed instructions for cooking this tasty meal. You need to follow these instructions in the given order.

- Mix the taco seasoning, tomato juice, and oil in a large shallow dish and stir well. Refrigerate the remaining 1/2 cup for basting. Turn the beef to coat it in the sauce. Refrigerate for a minimum of five hours after covering.

- Remove the beef from the marinade and discard it. Thread beef, peppers, onion, and tomatoes alternately on metal or soaked wooden skewers. Grill for 3 minutes on each side, uncovered, over medium heat. Brush with the marinade that has been set aside. Continue turning and basting till the meat is done to your liking, about 8-10 minutes. Serve with salsa de queso or sour cream, if desired.

4.17 Beef Suya

Preparation time

45 minutes

Servings

4 persons

Ingredients

We have listed below the ingredients that would be required by you for cooking the healthy and tasty meal:

- 2 tsp. ginger grounded
- One medium onion, cut into wedges
- 1 large tomato, cut into wedges
- Fresh cilantro leaves
- 1 tsp. red pepper flakes, crushed
- 1 tsp. garlic powder
- 1 roast beef tri-tip or beef top sirloin steak (2 lb.), sliced
- 1 cup salted peanuts
- 1 tablespoon paprika
- 2 teaspoons onion powder
- Two tbsp. canola oil
- One teaspoon salt

Instructions

Given below are the detailed instructions for cooking this tasty meal. You need to follow these instructions in the given order.

- Process the peanuts in a food processor until they are finely chopped.

- Pulse to combine pepper flakes, onion powder, paprika, ginger and garlic powder

- In a large bowl, place the beef. Drizzle with olive oil and season with salt. Toss to evenly coat. Toss in the peanut mixture and turn to coat. Refrigerate for 2 hours, covered. Drain the beef and toss out the marinade.

- Using soaked wooden skewers, thread the beef onto the skewers. Cover and grill over medium-high heat for 10-15 minutes or till beef attains desired doneness, turning occasionally. It can be served with onion, tomato, and cilantro before serving.

4.18 Cola Burgers

Preparation time

30 minutes

Servings

4 persons

Ingredients

We have listed below the ingredients that would be required by you for cooking the healthy and tasty meal:

- 1/2 cup saltines crushed (about 15)
- 1-1/2 pounds ground beef
- 6 hamburger buns, split
- 6 tbsp. French salad dressing
- 2 tbsp. Parmesan cheese grated
- 1 large egg
- 1/2 cup cola, divided
- 1/4 teaspoon salt

Instructions

Given below are the detailed instructions for cooking this tasty meal. You need to follow these instructions in the given order.

- Mix a quarter cup cola, egg, cracker crumbs, two tbsp salad dressing, Parmesan cheese and salt in a large mixing bowl. Mix in the beef crumbles thoroughly. Form six 3/4-inch-thick patties.

- Set aside the remaining cola as well as a salad dressing in a small bowl.

- Cover and cook burgers for three minutes on each side over medium heat. Then coat with the cola mixture. Continue grilling for another six to eight minutes, brushing as well as occasionally turning, until the desired doneness is reached. A thermometer must read 135°F for medium-rare.

- As desired, top burgers with optional toppings

4.19 Grilled Roast Beef Recipe

Preparation time

1hour

Servings

4 persons

Ingredients

We have listed below the ingredients that would be required by you for cooking the healthy and tasty meal:

- Three-pound beef roast

- cooking oil

- Salt and pepper to taste

Instructions

Given below are the detailed instructions for cooking this tasty meal. You need to follow these instructions in the given order.

- Turn the grill to high and wait fifteen to twenty minutes for it to heat up.

- The roast should be rubbed with oil. Season both sides with pepper and salt. If desired, additional seasoning can be added.

- Place the roast over direct heat when the grill is hot and sear each side for four to five minutes.

- Let the roast cook for around one hour on the grill for a medium-rare 2–3-pound roast. The grill should be heated to around 400 degrees Fahrenheit. Using a meat thermometer, check for doneness. It should be 145 degrees F for medium-rare.

- When the roast is about 5 degrees F below the desired temperature, remove it from the grill and set it aside for fifteen minutes before carving. As desired, carve and serve.

4.20 Perfectly Grilled Steak

Preparation time

30 minutes

Servings

4 persons

Ingredients

We have listed below the ingredients that would be required by you for cooking the healthy and tasty meal:

- Four one to one and a quarter-inch-thick boneless rib-eye

- Two tbsp canola or extra-virgin olive oil

- Kosher salt and freshly ground pepper

Instructions

Given below are the detailed instructions for cooking this tasty meal. You need to follow these instructions in the given order.

- Raise the temperature of the grill to high. Brush both sides of the steaks with oil and liberally season with salt and pepper. Put the steaks on a grill and cook for 4 to 5 minutes, or till light brown and a little charred. Turn the steaks over and cook for another 3–5 minutes for medium-rare (internal temperature of 135°F).

- Move the steaks to a cutting board and set them aside to rest for 5 minutes before slicing.

4.21 Grilled Cowboy Steak

Preparation time

3 hours 30 minutes

Servings

4 persons

Ingredients

We have listed below the ingredients that would be required by you for cooking the healthy and tasty meal:

- Twelve-pound bone-in rib-eye steak, about 2 1/2 inches thick
- Freshly ground black pepper
- Coarse salt
- Safflower oil or other neutral-tasting oil

Instructions

Given below are the detailed instructions for cooking this tasty meal. You need to follow these instructions in the given order.

- Allow 1 hour for the steak to rest at room temperature. Using paper towels, pat the steak dry. Preheat the grill to medium-high heat.
- When the grill is hot, scrub it with a grill brush and lightly oil it. Season both sides of the steak with salt and pepper, then place on the grill with the exposed bone covered in foil to prevent browning. Cover and cook for 5 minutes over direct heat. You also have to rotate the steak 45

degrees F halfway through for crosshatch marks; flip and cook for another 5 minutes.

- Cook for another 6 to 7 minutes per side on indirect heat, flipping once, for medium-rare (125 degrees F on an instant-read thermometer). Remove the steak from the grill and set it aside to rest for ten minutes prior to actually slicing and serving.

Conclusion

If you don't have the right equipment, outdoor cooking can at times be both exciting and challenging. Wood pellet grills, on the other hand, can help you improve your cooking skills and overall quality. For outdoor cooking, wood pellet grills are indispensable. You could use wood pellet grills to relax if you don't want to keep your hands busy too much because you're having a party. Several wood pellet grills don't even require your participation. A fireplace is built into the bottom of wood pellet grills. There's a grate on top of that which holds a water pan. Three to four additional grates will be available to cook your food on. Sausage clippings are also hung from the top of some grills. The thick ceramic wall keeps the temperature consistent throughout the smoker. Furthermore, you know exactly how much moisture your meat needs to stay moist. And most wood pellet grills have top and bottom airflow ducts that can be adjusted. As a result, you have complete control over the smoke and airflow. Another appealing feature of some grills is that they can be used as a grill and an oven for cooking pizza and baking. Even in cold climates, the thick ceramic wall provides great heat insulation for cooking. Grilling food on a wood fire pellet grill is simple and smoke-free. It's similar to a convection oven in that it evenly cooks food. Pellet grills and smokers also outperform traditional grilling methods because they produce less acrid smoke than traditional grills and smokers. Wood pellet grills provide versatility, flavor, and taste, as well as convenience and ease, value for money, and numerous health benefits. Switching to wood pellet

grilling is highly recommended for your health as well
as convenience.